FREEDOM FIRST

Brief Readings on Liberty,
Peace, and Prosperity

FREEDOM FIRST

Brief Readings on Liberty, Peace, and Prosperity

By Donald R. Chambers, PhD

Freedom First: Brief Readings on Liberty, Peace, and Prosperity

Printed in the United States of America

10 9 8 7 6 5 4 3 2 1

This book is a work of non-fiction. The author has made every effort to ensure that the accuracy of the information in this book was correct at time of publication. Neither the author nor the publisher nor any other person(s) associated with this book may be held liable for any damages that may result from any of the ideas made by the author in this book.

ISBN-13: 978-1-948035-15-6 (Hard Cover)
ISBN-13: 978-1-948035-20-0 (Paper Back)
ISBN-13: 978-1-948035-19-4 (eBook)

Library of Congress Control Number: 2018911262

Published by Defiance Press and Publishing, LLC

Bulk orders of this book may be obtained by contacting Defiance Press and Publishing, LLC at: www.defiancepress.com.

Public Relations Dept. – Defiance Press & Publishing, LLC
281-581-9300
pr@defiancepress.com

Defiance Press & Publishing, LLC
281-581-9300
info@defiancepress.com

*In memory of Gladstone Whitman who mentored
me in Austrian Economics and inspired me with his
strength and courage.*

TABLE OF CONTENTS

PREFACE

PEACE AND PROSPERITY ARE TWO of our most shared goals. This book is about obtaining peace and prosperity through liberty. It's about the incredible benefits of cooperation and the tremendous, though unintended, costs of coercion. If we appreciated these benefits and costs, humankind could experience harmony and prosperity that would allow us to surpass even the successes of the last few centuries, centuries during which we defeated smallpox and polio, slashed starvation rates, dramatically increased life expectancy, and reached the moon—figuratively and literally. But there's so much more we can do.

The philosophy underlying this book is that virtually everyone desires peace, health, prosperity, and the freedom to pursue happiness, but there's a primary obstacle to achieving this, which is that we tend to view initiating force or fraud as a necessary evil. Initiating force or fraud is such an accepted part of our culture that most people don't even see it. We're born into a society that presumes a need to initiate force against one another. Few people realize the extent to which they initiate force or fraud, or subconsciously support it, both in their personal lives and in their political positions. It takes careful thinking to overcome our knee-jerk reactions. But the wise find another way: walking in peace with one another.

The purpose of this book is to present a case for how we can continue to progress toward peaceful cooperation. I received advanced training in economics on my path to receiving a PhD in finance. But most of what I have learned about economics has come from my 36 years of research and teaching. Many of the readings in this book come from what I have learned and experienced in the finance and economics classes I've taught. I am grateful to the many students who were actively engaged in classroom discussions, who challenged my ideas, and who did so with great maturity and thoughtfulness.

1. You Never Forget How to Ride a Bicycle

I RECENTLY RODE A BICYCLE for the first time in years. In just a matter of minutes, I was able to navigate reasonably well. But, like everyone else, it took me many months as a child to learn how to ride a tricycle and graduate to a bicycle. The point is that remembering a skill is faster and easier than learning a skill for the first time. The same is true for learning how to navigate an economic system.

Riding a bicycle after many years is easy because of muscle memory. Of course, our muscles do not remember how to move; it is our brains that do the work. Muscle memory is a form of motor learning where our brains acquire the ability to repeat procedures automatically and without bringing our attention to the process.

In a free market, it takes a long time to understand how to thrive but, once we get the hang of it, our ability to recognize incentives and act on them becomes almost automatic. The same is true in a communist system. In communist countries, people learn how to select lines in which to stand, how to violate rules without being caught, how to avoid penalties, and how to extract favors.

During my years as a finance and economics professor, it has been difficult to teach international students, raised in a country with a long history of communism, the knowledge to thrive in a free market. For example, many of these students are reluctant to challenge their teachers openly. They have spent too many years in an environment where challenging the school's ideology was dangerous. For many of them, going to class involved taking notes and keeping quiet. Specific skills are necessary to thrive in free market systems and in totalitarian systems. But the skills are very different.

The same is true of socialism. The intelligentsia and political elitists attempt to comfort Americans about socialistic measures by pointing out economies that adopted similar measures and are doing "fine." It is true that socialist ideas often succeeded for extended periods. That is because good decision-making persists for a time after the proper incentives have been removed. It is like muscle memory. Even when healthy incentives in an economy have been removed, people go to work, strive to improve efficiency, and take pride in their work. It takes a while for it to all fall apart. Venezuela is a clear and tragic example.

In Orwell's classic work, Animal Farm, the stages of change are much like those in Venezuela: the government takes over some of the economy's decision-making, productivity declines, the ruling party blames political enemies, and the cycle repeats itself with the government increasing its control over another part of the economy. The socialist government in Venezuela keeps taking the wealth created from private ownership in previous times and using it to try to keep the socialist system going as it expands its control over the economy. Venezuela can still turn back, but it will be difficult.

An engineer named Destin Sandlin created a bicycle with a sort of "backward" steering mechanism. It moves left when the handlebars are turned clockwise (right) and right when the handlebars are turned counterclockwise (left). Experienced bicycle riders have a hard time adjusting to the bicycle despite fully understanding the change. As in the case of the backward bicycle, switching between economic systems involves learning which skills need to be reversed and which can be left unchanged.

Though less far along than Venezuela, America has been on the path to socialism for about 100 years. In some areas of our country, most residents rely on welfare, and their families have done so for multiple generations. If America ever attempts to return to the principles on which it thrived, it will be a difficult and contentious journey. For the people living in regions of economic decay, the muscle memory will be hard to unlearn.

2. A FAILURE TO COMMUNICATE

WE ALL LEARNED A LOT about personal communication in small groups as we grew up. We learned that we gather information about what the people around us want by listening, and by studying facial responses and body language. How did I know my brother liked swordfish more than mackerel? Easy: I listened to him order swordfish and watched him enjoy eating it.

But how do hundreds of millions of people communicate their needs and preferences in a modern economy? How does a national pizza chain learn whether the value of developing a new style of pizza is worth the cost? Obviously, they don't do it just through listening in on conversations and watching people eat pizza. Sure, marketing people run focus groups in which they observe a few people through one-way mirrors, but most of the signals that drive a modern economy transmit themselves through markets—through sales volume and market prices. Farmers plant crops based on commodity prices (when government doesn't interfere with the price signals through subsidies). Miners make plans based on the prices of ores and various metals. The same concept holds for energy producers, tech firms, financial institutions, etc.

Entrepreneurs and other value creators see market prices as opportunities. Can I make something that will retail for a price that exceeds its production costs ? Can I figure out a way to produce my product at a lower cost? Market prices are offers to exchange, and it is through the benefits of exchange that we thrive. Markets will crush many of our dreams, but most ideas need to be crushed. Markets crushed my idea of owning a restaurant chain. Markets crushed my idea of being a professional athlete. But markets will also guide us to the best use of our abilities. Markets guided me toward being a finance professor and investment consultant.

Every day, markets guide millions of people into making crucial decisions such as whether to attend college and which car to buy. And market prices guide over 300 million Americans each day in making billions of tiny decisions such as paper or plastic, regular or premium, lobster or catfish, hand-sewn or machine-stitched, pay-per-view or broadcast TV, leather or rubber soles, long or short showers, whether to set the air conditioner on high or low, and so on. Supply and demand do the talking in a free market.

And those who listen to the information in market prices can use that information to better help others. Take, for example, pizza chains that create new products when (and only when) customers are willing to pay more for them than the chain must spend to get the pizza out the door. When we listen to markets and react to the information they signal, we find out what people really want and decide how we can meet those wants using less resources than the next guy. Apple, one of the biggest firms in the world, is a great example of an organization serving others by meeting consumer demand and doing so cost-effectively. The media glorifies small, struggling farms and starving artists, but businesses and people that spend more than they make are often doing little to benefit others. What we have there is a failure to communicate.

3. Buying Local Sends False Signals

Buying local means buying from people who live close to you, even if it means paying higher prices or accepting lower quality. In some cases, such as getting fresher produce, it might mean buying from producers with shorter delivery times. But, when freshness doesn't matter, buying local means restricting our opportunities to trade, and the more we restrict opportunities to trade, the more we limit the benefits of trade and competition. When our behavior limits competition, it limits the incentives to innovate and become more efficient.

Put differently, buying local for the sake of buying local means lying to your neighbors and rewarding incompetence. Sure, we might not mean to lie, but that's what our behavior amounts to. Suppose I buy a candle for $10 from a local supplier, even though I could have bought a better candle for $8 from a distant supplier. I have lied to my neighbor. I've told my neighbor, "You make a great candle and you sell it at a great price. Keep up the good work." More honest would be to buy the $8 candle and send $2 to the local supplier with a message that reads, "Hi, neighbor. I like you. But your candles are overpriced and inferior by comparison. Even though you live closer to me and have lower shipping costs, you can't compete on any basis other than guilt. So I'm sending you this gift in the hopes that you'll improve your candles, become more efficient, or find something else to do that better serves your fellow humans."

Buying overpriced products based on affinity rewards incompetence. Buying local implies that neighbors deserve to be treated better than distant strangers.

It also signals to people like the candle maker that they're doing business in the best way possible. When merchants make money only because their community is doing them a favor, they don't have the signal that leads them to think: *I have to work harder and smarter, so my neighbors won't have to make sacrifices to keep me in business.* Instead, they're led to think: *No changes necessary.*

It's not just the neighbors who've already set up shop that we're lying to. We're doing it to the neighbors who might be deciding whether to start a new business or to accept a job offer. We're telling our neighbors they should start a candle business, or they should start a career working at a candle company. Markets are a vital communication system in a society. Let's communicate wisely and honestly.

In psychology, holding two conflicting beliefs is called cognitive dissonance. In economics, buying local because it's local, and receiving self-esteem from being economically successful, should be called economic dissonance. The reason is this: we take pleasure in believing that the people who utilize our services do so because we are good at what we do. But, if we all give preference to locals, there is no reason to believe we are good at what we do; it just means that we are local. In my experience, the intelligentsia have no problem with holding mutually contradictory beliefs.

4. CARRYING WATER IS HARD WORK IF DONE ALONE

YEARS AGO, I BEGAN MOST semesters with a challenge to my students. On the first day of class, I would schedule a contest for day two, with the winner receiving extra credit. I would bring a large container of water to class and place it on a table on one side of the room. All the students would have a chance to carry as much water as they could from one side of the room to the other in a single trip. They were allowed to bring one container of their choosing. There was only one rule: the container had to be made with no direct or indirect help from any other person. In other words, students could not use the benefits of exchange to carry the water. They truly had to do it alone.

Students were slow in grasping the meaning of this one simple rule. Some students showed up with large buckets, indicating the extent to which they took for granted the services provided by people who made and sold the containers to them. The students who eventually realized the severity of the one simple rule did not even try to transport the water.

For those students who did try, some of the best ideas were sponges, hollowed gourds, and crude baskets woven from large, green leaves. Yet these containers were often obtained with help from exchange: the sponges were purchased, rather than harvested, and the gourds were hollowed with purchased knives.

I used water as the object of the contest for two important reasons. First, immediate access to water is critical to survival. Second, the ability to transport water allows a person to hunt and gather further from a home site. More fundamentally, the point of the exercise was to give the students a vivid lesson in the importance of trade. It is a shame academics and politicians do not participate in this exercise. If they did, they would have a lot less disdain for those who facilitate trade.

5. THE RISE OF PREPPERS AND THEIR LACK OF CONFIDENCE IN SOCIETY

WHAT WOULD HAPPEN IF THE economy completely collapsed? Most people would die in a matter of months without being able to replenish their food, water, energy products, and medical supplies. Most people seem uninterested in understanding what prevents an economy from collapsing. Few worry that the economy will collapse.

There is one exception: preppers. Preppers are people who devote incredible amounts of time and energy in preparing for doomsday. *Doomsday Preppers* on the National Geographic Channel documents the bizarre ways some people think about and prepare for social and economic collapse. They usually obsess about a particular risk such as a nuclear attack, the power grid going down, a devastating storm, civil unrest, an earthquake, a tsunami, or a pandemic. They emphasize these risks because they view society as held together by a fragile system of law and order without which there would be immediate and universal looting and rioting.

But the robustness of our institutions—our systems of law and order, as well as our faith in those institutions—should not be underestimated. Historical evidence indicates our institutions are quite robust. They have withstood major power outages such as the Great Northeast Blackout of 1965 that affected more than 30 million people. They've survived earthquakes, hurricanes, and outbreaks of disease. I suspect that, in all cases, some people looted and stole in the ensuing confusion. But, in most or all such events, people focused on meeting the challenges and helping one another. I have fond recollections of cooperation among residents during the 1972 hurricane that struck my hometown of Corning, New York. It was similar to New York City after Hurricanes Sandy and Katrina. Desperate times often bring out the best in people: in their broad view of their own self-interest, they understand that peaceful cooperation almost always generates better outcomes than belligerent violence.

Both coercion and cooperation exist in large societies. Preppers focus on the power of violent coercion but neglect the powerful force of peaceful cooperation. Not just preppers, but all of us, underestimate the power and benefits of cooperation—not just between family, friends, and lovers, but even between people who do not know or like each other.

Cooperation and self-interest keep us alive not just in good times but even in bad times. We are best able to get food, clothing, and shelter when we cooperate—and societies with good institutions tend to cooperate well.

6. COME ON DOWN—THE PRICE IS RIGHT!

STUDENTS BEGIN MY COURSE THINKING markets are predictable and, at times, quite irrational. So I play a quick guessing game with them. I tell them I'm thinking of the market value of something, and I want them to guess the amount. It's like *The Price Is Right,* except they don't know what the item is and there are no prizes. After each guess, I tell them whether the guess was too high or too low. The goal is to get to the secret value in as few guesses as possible.

Each semester, the pattern of guesses is similar. The first guess is usually around $20. I tell them, "Too low." The next few guesses rapidly escalate as I tell them each guess is too low: $100, $1,000, $100,000, $1 million, $100 million, $10 billion. Finally the guess hits hundreds of billions of dollars, or even a trillion dollars, and I tell them, "Too high." The guesses then quickly home in on the true figure: $50 billion.

I sketched a diagram of their answers, and it looks something like this:

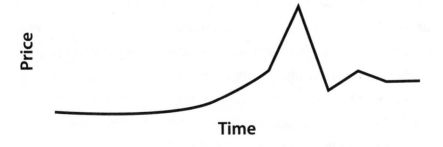

The item I chose was a successful and mature US corporation. Such a firm begins as a tiny venture worth relatively little. As time progresses, most ventures fail, but a few succeed. If highly successful, a firm's market value skyrockets and its value soars in anticipation of more good news. At some point, every firm's growth slows. Eventually, the market value of the firm falls to a more moderate level as investors accept the limits of the firm's growth potential. The pattern of prices through time that emerges from the classroom guessing game mirrors what's often seen in the financial market's valuation of stocks. Some people call it a price bubble.

The primary point of the exercise is to show that the bubble-like price patterns aren't generated by emotions or stupidity. The guesses are reasonable—especially since pricing an asset of uncertain worth is very difficult, whether it's a professor's imaginary asset or a business venture. Investors respond to market signals just like my "too high" and "too low" clues. In retrospect, the prices often miss the mark, but that doesn't imply a bubble.

Yet some economists claim they can predict patterns and prove that traders are acting irrationally. They claim that financial markets produce bubbles and that market values are so unreliable that it justifies government regulation by the political elite.

Federal Reserve Chairman Alan Greenspan famously described the stock market as exhibiting "irrational exuberance" in December 1996 when the Dow Jones Industrial Average was around 6,500. But the Dow has been consistently above that level ever since, recently reaching about four times that level. If Greenspan participated in my classroom guessing game, would he really do better than my students? If Greenspan was so much smarter than other investors at guessing the right stock prices, it seems he should have based his career on his investing prowess rather than becoming a consultant and government employee.

7. If It Walks Like a Duck and Quacks Like a Duck....

STUDENTS HAVE BECOME MORE AND more reluctant to speak out in their classes. American institutions of higher education have become some of the least tolerant places in America. Freedom of speech as we know it no longer exists on many college campuses. Students with good intentions are afraid to make honest, factual statements if those statements contradict the beliefs of the enforcers of political correctness. For example, the FBI reported that, in 2015, about 90 percent of black murder victims were killed by other blacks. Most students would be wise not to make such a statement, even if the students' comments were clearly made in the context of providing insight into how to address the problem of crime. The rules of political correctness extend beyond race. For example, it is okay to note that about 90 percent of murders are done by males, but it is not okay to cite the fact that men are about nine times more likely to be victims of murder than women.

But academic intolerance is not new. In the centuries prior to the Renaissance, academic institutions were dominated by scholasticism—a system of learning based on unchallengeable propositions and rigidly formalized debate. As the system evolved, some academic institutions soared in prestige and power. As Lord Acton famously wrote, "Power tends to corrupt and absolute power corrupts absolutely. Great men are almost always bad men." As the prestige of these academic institutions increased, their intolerance for dissent continued to grow.

Some of the leading academic institutions reached the point of demanding that all students agree to the institution's list of supposed truths. For example, in some institutions, students were not allowed to question Aristotle's conclusions; in many others, they were not allowed to question Christian tenets. While Aristotle should certainly be commended for his contributions to philosophy and science, some of his beliefs are now universally understood to be false. Yet applicants who failed to accept these ideas were sometimes denied admission. Worse, students that voiced disagreement risked expulsion.

College campuses today have reached a similar sorry state. There are reasonable and factually correct statements that simply are not tolerated on many campuses today. Generally, one may not say anything positive about wealthy white men or anything negative about the poor, nonwhites and women.

One of my daughters took a college class in which the professor exhibited this intolerance. The professor challenged the students to consider a male friend of his who did not feel like a male. The professor said, "If my friend walks down the street dressed like a woman, acts like a woman, and thinks of himself as a woman, who can claim he is anything other than a woman?" To that, my daughter asked, "If I walk on all fours like a kitten, purr like a kitten, and drink milk from a saucer, does that make me a kitten?" I am proud of her. But that sort of response wasn't good for her GPA. Despite their pious claims, most faculty reward students for writing essays that parrot back the professors' political beliefs and punish them for challenging the professors' beliefs. Academia is no place for the free exchange of ideas.

8. It's Almost Midnight to Some

THE DOOMSDAY CLOCK BEGAN IN the late 1940s, spawned as a publicity stunt by scientists who helped pioneer the use of atomic weapons in World War II. The clock has been used by the Bulletin of Atomic Scientists to signal the world's nearness to devastating nuclear war. The scientists adjust the clock periodically to communicate their opinion as to when the world becomes more dangerous or less dangerous. The closer the clock is to midnight, the closer the world supposedly is to nuclear war. I remember the incredible focus of America in the early 1960s on civil preparedness for a nuclear attack by the Soviets. The Doomsday Clock haunted me as a child.

While I remain concerned about the dangers of nuclear war, I dismiss the ability of these so-called scientists to forecast the danger. I believe their forecasts are based on political opinions rather than reason and evidence.

In 1980, the clock showed seven minutes to Doomsday. By 1984, especially because of the election of the "evil" Ronald Reagan, the time remaining had diminished to three minutes shy of midnight. In a clear shock to the scientific intelligentsia, the "war-mongering" Reagan actually diminished the danger, and the clock moved 14 minutes away from danger during 1984 to 1991.

In 2007, a strange thing happened. After 60 years of a focus on war as the paramount threat to humanity, scientists discovered a bigger threat: global warming! They began using global warming as an excuse for their fear mongering and began to include global warming in setting the time on their Doomsday Clock. But wait, isn't this the publicity tool of the Bulletin of Atomic Scientists? Were they acquired by some society of global-warming scientists? What do scientists fearful of nuclear war have in common with scientists studying global warming? Fear—and the use of fear—to push the political agenda of the intellectual elitists. The so-called scientists were able to convince themselves the clock should be set to three minutes from midnight in 2015.

In 2016, the unthinkable happened: Donald Trump was elected president. Nuclear war and global warming were now inevitable in the scientists' politicized minds. But with the clock already set to three minutes to midnight, how could they evoke sufficient fear? For the first time, the clock was advanced by a fraction of a minute (a half minute) rather than by one or more whole minutes. Why? Did they believe their perceived catastrophe of electing Trump was worth only a fraction of a minute? I think not. My guess is that, with three minutes left, they could announce only two more one-minute moves driven by fear mongering. By switching to fractions of a minute, they reserved plenty of dry powder (fear mongering) for the approaching 2020 elections.

In 2018, they advanced the clock by another thirty seconds to two minutes remaining. They cited climate change and "the downward spiral of nuclear rhetoric between US President Donald Trump and North Korean Supreme Leader Kim Jong-un" as factors. (Wrong again!) About the same time, the organization's chair stepped down in the midst of a potential professional doomsday of his own—I wonder if he saw that coming!

9. Life, Liberty and the Pursuit of Happiness

I often ask my students what they think the Declaration of Independence means when it says all men "are created equal." Does that mean a person like me is physically equal to LeBron James or mentally equal to Albert Einstein? The answer is obvious to those few students who know the words that come next in the Declaration of Independence: "that they are endowed by their Creator with certain inalienable rights, that among these rights are life, liberty and the pursuit of happiness." The Founding Fathers knew that we are not mentally or physically equal. Rather, they were proclaiming the revolutionary idea that we are equally entitled to our rights.

So I am free to pursue a career in the NBA or to try to write a unified theory of physics. Simply put, the Founders were laying the foundation for a nation that would strive to make each person equal under the law. Coming from a shared history of a world in which kings were declared as directly speaking the word of God, this was a radical, innovative, and bold experiment. Ronald Reagan wondered aloud how "that little band of men so advanced beyond their time that the world has never seen their like since, evolve the idea that you and I have within ourselves the God-given right and the ability to determine our own destiny."

Now the intelligentsia and political elites are trying to achieve equality of outcomes and, in doing this, they are taking away our rights to equal treatment under the law and to determine our own destinies. The only way government can ensure that I can compete equally against LeBron James in basketball or Albert Einstein in theoretical physics is to somehow destroy or constrain their abilities to excel. Kurt Vonnegut covered this point wonderfully and humorously in his short story, "Harrison Bergeron." Vonnegut described the handicapper general's efforts to bring ballet dancers and newscasters down to the skill levels of the least qualified citizens.

We can have equality of outcomes or equal treatment under the law. We can only pick one. If America picks equality of outcomes, it will ensure no one will have an incentive to invest in the future, innovate, or work hard. The pie could, in principle, be divided into equal pieces. But the pie would get smaller through time as the lack of incentives to maintain and innovate our production capabilities would lead to decay and obsolescence.

Furthermore, some of the pie would need to be set aside to compensate for the inevitable corruption that enables the decadent lifestyles of the political elites of authoritarian regimes with weak private property rights. But the pie will necessarily get smaller and smaller. Just watch North Korea shrink and starve while South Korea flourishes. Watch Venezuelans suffer from a government unable to pump oil out of the ground. That is the future the intellectual and political elitists wish for America, which is why they never criticize the policies or leaders of those repressive regimes.

10. Borderline Disorder

THE DEBATE OVER IMMIGRATION IN recent years is a disgrace. The progressive left sets forth an entirely untenable position: the immigrants who bypassed the legal immigration process are not here illegally; they simply lack documentation. They hold that all undocumented immigrants should be protected and allowed to progress toward citizenship. This is unquestionably an "open borders" position.

I have raised this issue with numerous supporters of "undocumented immigrants," and I have yet to receive a cogent response. None of them have responded: "Yes, I understand that my position is tantamount to open borders, but I am convinced that everyone in the world should be allowed to come to America and that we should allow them to benefit from our social programs." None have said, "We can handle it; we must make this sacrifice." The universal response has been to switch topics, typically to rehash the burdens faced by these people who "lack documentation." How can any sane American think that an open border policy would work?

Can there be a single, rational person who believes that an open border policy makes sense for America? Open borders mean that anyone who wants to and is able to make the journey can become a full US citizen, which includes full access to America's plethora of social giveaways, safety nets, and social programs. Can you imagine the hordes that would rush into America, knowing that all the benefits and opportunities in America would be available to them? There would be literally over a hundred million needy people within a few years, all in a hurry lest the door slam shut! The golden goose would be crushed both for existing citizens and future legal immigrants.

Instead of having a healthy discussion of this difficult issue, we find ourselves enmeshed in a web of discourse and deceit. Liberals accuse conservatives of opposing all immigration. Furthermore, they refuse to acknowledge that their own opposition to any immigration controls is tantamount to supporting open borders. America effectively had open borders many decades ago, but that was before it established the massive social programs that allow immigrants to come to the US and live off the government.

People that jump fences to attend athletic events or concerts are not undocumented attendees. They are illegal attendees. I cannot recollect ever meeting an American who opposed all immigration. Those I have met who oppose illegal immigration are highly in favor of a well-regulated system of legal immigration; yet progressive leftists are succeeding in promulgating their claim that this is a debate between those who favor immigration and those who oppose it.

11. WHAT EXACTLY IS IN THAT PRICE?

STUDENTS ENTER MY CLASS BELIEVING that oil companies are to blame for environmental damage such as oil spills and carbon emissions. Years ago, I attended a seminar at a liberal arts college conducted by a world-famous economist. At one point, the economist commented that government-levied fines on corporations, such as those levied against oil companies after an oil spill, are paid for by consumers in the long run, not corporate shareholders. Many of the students and faculty were outraged, viewing it as a pro-corporate political position. But most well-trained economists think that that statement derives from a simple economic principle: businesses need to pass on their costs to their customers to stay in business.

In deciding whether to embark on a venture, businesses evaluate all possible outcomes. Oil companies must include in their cost-benefit analysis all the things that could go wrong—dry wells, drilling accidents, spills during transportation, refinery fires, government penalties, government fines, and so on—ensuring that they can charge enough for the product to cover the expected costs and earn enough in profit to reward their risk-taking.

When governments institute larger fines for environmentally harmful events such as oil spills, it causes businesses to institute safety measures to reduce the probability of accidents. To stay in business, companies must receive enough revenue to cover the expected costs of financing those additional safety measures, along with enough money to pay the expected costs of future fines, given that perfectly safe transportation of oil is simply not possible. In the long run, businesses pass on these costs, like all other costs of production, to their customers in the form of higher prices. These higher prices signal information otherwise unknown to most consumers so they can decide if the products' benefits warrant the added costs.

An easier example to understand is a small retail business, such as a convenience store or a sandwich shop. In order to be sustainable, store owners must include all expected costs in setting the prices they charge. Therefore, it is ultimately the customers of those stores that pay for shoplifting, employee theft, product spoilage, business taxes, business insurance, and all the other normal costs of running that business. When someone steals from a store, they are actually stealing from its customers.

Even if it can be argued that some costs are not passed on to consumers, they are not paid for by corporations. No corporation has ever borne the pain of paying corporate taxes, paying jury verdicts, or paying fines. Corporations are just legal constructs through which people transact. It may not be obvious who really suffers those losses in the short run: shareholders, employees, or consumers. But, in the long run, shareholders pass all anticipated expenses on to consumers.

Most of my students realize that it is the consumers of a product who determine how much product is produced. For example, it is just common sense that the people who buy products harvested from endangered species are ultimately to blame for the animals being killed. Ultimately, it is the consumers who determine which products will be produced, how much will be produced, and how much environmental damage will occur. So each person's responsibility for environmental damage is best measured by how much they consume. Do we really think that political leaders and Hollywood actors use less transportation and other energy-consuming products than the ordinary person?

12. SELF-DRIVING CARS

FOR YEARS I HAVE BEEN saddened and concerned about the death and injury toll from car and truck accidents. In the 1960s, the annual fatality count in the US from such accidents averaged more than 50,000, roughly the same as the total fatalities of the US military from the entire Vietnam War (about 58,000). Despite large long-term population increases in the US and increased mileage driven by each driver (until recently), the annual death rate has come down thanks to safer cars, better highways, and tighter controls over drunk driving. In 2017, there were about 40,000 fatalities.

I predicted years ago that something would be done about this unacceptable level of death and injury via automobile. I predicted self-driving cars. I predicted that the solution was "smart highways" that used electronic signals to guide cars to stay in their lanes and avoid collisions. I was right about the timeframe but wrong about the solution. Like others, I never anticipated that the solution would largely come from electronics on each vehicle that functioned independently—much like humans—in perceiving the surrounding conditions and driving the car appropriately.

We are on the verge of unleashing the ability of self-driving vehicles to free drivers from the mindless task of vigilance while, at the same time, generating enormous improvements in safety. There is no doubt in my mind that driverless trucks will be making long-distance hauls through the night, commuters will be able to get work done on their daily commutes, and operator-less cars will lead shared transportation services to tremendous economic efficiencies and reduced traffic congestion.

There is only one thing that can substantially delay the inevitable: the coercive power of government. There is no doubt that government will cause innumerable deaths and costs by standing in the way of this breakthrough rather than heartily supporting it. First, the coercive power of our legal system will penalize progress by levying massive damage awards even when it becomes clear that the driverless systems, although imperfect, are safer than human operation.

Second, the government will continue to be incredibly uncooperative in aiding progress in this area. Specifically, there are low-cost, easy improvements to roads and highways that can facilitate and expedite the transition to self-driving cars, such as installing small electronic devices in traffic signals and elsewhere that communicate with driverless cars. The various governmental organizations that made almost zero progress in developing smart highways have not and will not be capable of providing even a tiny amount of cooperation to help facilitate the use of driverless cars.

The roadblocks to progress erected by various levels of government throughout the US will be entirely responsible for tens of thousands of unnecessary traffic deaths—perhaps several hundred thousand deaths in the US—over the next decade. The policy of holding back advances until they are found by the government to be foolproof, as in the case of the FDA, will be arrogantly maintained despite the tragic losses of life during the period in which driverless cars are outlawed, even when they are proven safer than human-operated cars, but far enough from perfect to give bureaucrats the excuse to cover their butts by standing in the way of progress.

13. THE TRAGEDY OF THE COMMONS

FREE MARKETS AND PRIVATE PROPERTY rights are the foundations of almost all of the technological advances that have led to incredible economic benefits most of us enjoy today—benefits that nobody, even royalty, enjoyed in previous centuries. More fundamentally, private property rights and economic liberty are essential to modern commerce and are, therefore, essential to the principles used to understand corporate finance, investments, and other such subjects.

I extol the virtues of private property rights and free markets to my students. Many of them jump to the conclusion that I am a conservative, or at least a Republican. I am neither. I point out that I believe marijuana and prostitution should be decriminalized. Unfortunately, that leads many of the students to believe I am—at a minimum—a libertine, and quite likely an old pervert. I object to being viewed as a libertine. A libertine is a person who behaves with loose morals. In my case, not much could be further from the truth. I do not "smoke, drink or chew, or go with girls that do."

To many of my students, I am an enigma. How can a person that does not drink alcohol, smoke cigarettes, smoke marijuana, or consort with prostitutes support the idea that these activities should be legal? Most people believe that everything they dislike should be illegal and everything they like should be legal.

Everybody wants sewage plants to protect our waterways from pollution. But nobody wants a sewage plant near their home. Similarly, everybody wants to be able to do the things they like to do, but nobody wants others to do things of which they disapprove.

Almost everyone agrees that government has become too large and too powerful and is spending too much money. But people stridently object to any reduction in government that restricts something they enjoy.

Our collective drive to increase the power and size of government is a form of the "tragedy of the commons": the idea that people will abuse a resource if they bear only part of the harm from losing that resource. For example, each community wants federal money to fund its pet projects. The tax burden of that spending falls on all communities—not just the community receiving the federal funds. Every community fights for a share of federal funds. The result is that many pet projects get funded, and the huge tax burden falls on everyone—potentially making everyone worse off. If each community really believed their pet project was worth its cost, they should fund it themselves.

Instead, we experience the tragedy of the commons. Similarly, when one group of people pushes for a law to make actions they dislike illegal, they are making themselves better off. Then another group pushes for their favorite law, and so on. We end up with so many rules that everyone is worse off.

The breadth and depth of federal regulations and spending have soared. Each year when I drive by Washington, DC, I see more and more office buildings, more and more superhighways, and more and more cars. Housing prices in Washington, DC rose even in 2009! The reason is simple: the tragedy of the commons means the US government is growing out of control, leading lobbyists, contractors, and legal firms to create ever-larger footprints near the epicenter of federal power.

Even prior to the tragic Hurricane Maria in 2017, Puerto Rico was in desperate shape. Puerto Rico was paying the price for decades of out-of-control spending and borrowing. Half of its citizens were on Medicaid (compared to 20 percent elsewhere in the United States). One way or another, like Puerto Rico and Venezuela, there will be a tragic episode for the US mainland if it remains on the course of ever-expanding local, state, and federal government. The questions are when, how, and how bad will the devastation be when it occurs?

14. Don't Tread on My Rights

I use the words coercion and force interchangeably in this book. What do they mean? It's not straightforward. I often ask my students: does an employer use coercion when he or she fires an incompetent worker? Is a student using coercion when he or she ends a bad friendship or relationship? We usually find common ground on the idea that terminating a bad relationship—especially a personal one—is not coercion if the aggrieved party has no right to be in the relationship.

Let's examine a difficult scenario. Is an employer using coercion when he or she fires an employee solely because she doesn't like the way the employee expresses his or her religious opinions at work? My students are nearly unanimous in thinking the employer is using coercion and has no right to do so because firing the worker violates the employee's right to religious freedom. I then ask if they someday run a household, should they have the right to get rid of a plumber or babysitter who spouts off offensive religious views while they're working. Students are nearly unanimous again, but this time they assert their right as homeowners to get rid of the worker. On what basis do the students award stronger property rights to homeowners than business owners? Is there a fair and logical way to make these types of distinctions?

A theme throughout this book is that it's wrong for anyone to initiate, or threaten to initiate, coercion. But we need to define coercion to communicate clearly. I won't attempt to define the word coercion in a way everyone will agree with but, rather, how I use it in this book:

Coercion is infringing (or threatening to infringe) on a natural right of another person.

The above definition of coercion then begs the question: how do you define a natural right? A natural right is what a person is entitled to if they lived independently in every respect except for when they interact in mutually agreeable ways. The most fundamental natural rights are the right of every person to control their own bodies, their own lives, the fruits of their labor, and to trade with others freely.

Let's suppose a man named Dave labors on a vegetable garden at his home and receives three threats:

Ann, Dave's girlfriend, threatens to end their relationship unless she gets a tomato.

Beth, Dave's employer, threatens to fire Dave unless she gets a tomato.

Carol, a stranger to Dave, threatens to damage Dave's garden unless she gets a tomato.

Dave has a natural right to the tomatoes because he grew them using his own labor in his own garden. But Dave does not have a natural right to a relationship with Ann or to be employed by Beth unless they consent. Dave has no right—only a privilege—to a particular job or a particular relationship. No matter how much Dave values his relationship with Ann or his employment with Beth, he is not being coerced by Ann or Beth. If Dave had a right to the job and to the relationship, then that would imply that Ann and Beth had no right to choose with whom they wished to associate. Only Carol is using coercion. Only Carol is threatening to violate one of Dave's natural rights—in this case, his right to enjoy the benefits of his garden.

This seemingly trivial distinction between a privilege and a right is the crux of a huge divide. Throughout America, citizens are asserting privileges as rights. We can all agree that a girlfriend who threatens to terminate a relationship with a boyfriend if he does not agree to accompany her to a party on Saturday is not using coercion. But we should also agree that it is not coercion when an employer requires someone to work on Saturdays by threatening to fire them. Without a contract to the contrary, an employee does not have a right to continued employment. Regardless of the circumstances, strangers have no right to other people's belongings. The intelligentsia violate the concept of natural rights freely when redistributing other people's wealth, but my experience is that they believe quite strongly in their rights to keep their property.

15. WHAT ON EARTH IS THE NOOSPHERE?

WHEN I BEGAN MY CAREER as a finance professor, the personal computer had just begun to penetrate the workplace. The problem with using a personal computer was losing access to the central depository of data tapes and software available when using a terminal to a mainframe. I never imagined that, years later, the internet would emerge, and PCs would provide access to an enormous cloud of data and software that would dwarf the mainframes of thirty years ago.

Personal electronic devices and the internet have accelerated the progress of the noosphere, a concept described by Vladimir Vernadsky about 100 years ago. Vernadsky described the Earth as developing in three stages: a stage of inanimate development as the planet took its physical form, a stage of biological development as life forms evolved, and a stage called the noosphere, in which cognition evolves such that people throughout the world increasingly share similar knowledge and information.

We live at an incredible point in the noosphere where more and more people have instant access to vast quantities of knowledge about things such as current events and other facts, and people have the ability to profit from others' skills and education. Information is instantly and costlessly exchanged throughout the world using the internet and increasingly affordable personal electronic devices. In some ways, we can feel overwhelmed with the quantity of information available and the speed with which it is changing.

We are also increasingly able to communicate in real time with people throughout the world with texts, photos, and even videos. When I attend conferences that feature well-known speakers, I notice there are people in the audience competing to distribute the speaker's comments throughout the world using Twitter and other instantaneous social media. They are listening to the speaker, but also instantly connecting with millions of others outside the room who share similar interests.

In terms of commerce, people in retail stores comparison-shop electronically by consulting online prices and reviews. And reviews are becoming powerful indicators of quality, with systems emerging to ensure that reviews are legitimate and unbiased through verifications and published reputations. This incredible worldwide access to information on product quality and price will drive gains in meeting consumer preferences quickly and efficiently.

The amount of available information may seem overwhelming. However, each of us individually only needs a tiny portion of the available information to be efficient at our economic tasks. One reason that our information needs are limited is that much of the key information we need to share directly with each other is captured in market prices. Market prices are signals of how to cooperate with each other. Are you unsure how to best provide a useful good or service to your fellow humans? You do not need to learn about every item or every person in the world. All you need to do is find a product you can sell at a market price that leaves you a profit. Finding and using opportunities to trade at market prices that satisfy your desire to consume and reward your ability to produce is the way to serve both yourself and others.

The collapse of the USSR and the need for reforms of the Chinese economy were driven in substantial part by the inability of their centrally planned economies to keep pace with free market economies and the increasing speed at which technology changed. Famines have been a natural part of life throughout most of history. But, by the 1970s, the impending food shortages of both the Soviets and Chinese became unacceptable in a world in which most countries had abundant food.

In North Korea, not only do the people still suffer from shortages, they are kept in the dark, taught that life is worse elsewhere in the world, and that their current struggles are the result of aggression by the United States and South Korea. But, as technology advances, access to information is becoming less expensive and more difficult for the government to suppress. How long can the North Korean people be kept down?

Most Americans have had limited exposure to the stories of those who suffered under communism. Our media ignores the tyrannies performed by socialists and communists. But there is a free market in information evolving. Increasingly people are sharing information directly with each other through social media, although nations such as China do not allow access to websites that others take for granted. But, in most economies, information control is no longer the domain of a few major media outlets and the intelligentsia. As access to information expands throughout the world, everyone will understand the inability of central planning to meet the challenges of modern economies.

16. ROSCOE FILBURN AND INTERSTATE COMMERCE

HOW DID AMERICA GET TO the point that the federal government inserts itself so deeply into the economic affairs of its citizens? It wasn't always that way. Almost all my students view the massive and intrusive activities of the federal government as if they've always existed and were authorized by the Constitution.

The power of the federal government to regulate and tax our economic activities has been expanded through a series of crucial decisions by the Supreme Court, many of which occurred during the FDR administration. These decisions emboldened officials to take huge leaps from the limited federal powers envisioned by the Founding Fathers. The focal point of the debate over the constitutionality of the new laws was the interstate commerce clause of the Constitution. The interstate commerce clause gives Congress the power to "regulate commerce...among the several states."

Two key points that *The Federalist Papers* made clear were that

(1) the regulations the Founders had in mind would encourage free trade (not inhibit it), and (2) that the trade to be regulated was that between residents of one state and another. But the Supreme Court has allowed Congress to increase its power through a very expansive view of this clause. The courts have surrendered to Congress the power to regulate any economic action by one or more persons that could conceivably have an effect on anyone from another state.

Federal intrusion into our economic lives began in earnest in the early 1900s. But the defining moment happened in 1942. The Supreme Court upheld the constitutionality of a federal law that prevented an Ohio farmer named Roscoe Filburn from growing wheat on his own property for use by his own livestock. The federal law was enacted in an attempt to "stabilize" market prices. The court ruled that the farmer's wheat production altered interstate trade because it enabled the farmer to feed his livestock without buying grain from the marketplace, which, in turn, could affect market prices and hence people in other states. Based on the Supreme Court's decision, the federal government could now regulate virtually any economic action by any citizen since, in theory, any such action could affect a person in another state. The absurdity is that the interstate commerce clause was being used to discourage commerce rather than encourage it, as originally intended.

In 2012, Chief Justice John Roberts set a new standard for expanded interpretations of the Constitution's interstate commerce clause to support intrusive federal regulations. Opponents of Obamacare had argued that Americans have the right to choose not to buy health insurance. They argued that, while prevailing constitutional law gives the federal government the power to regulate economic activities, the interstate commerce clause does not give it the right to force people to engage in economic activities. Specifically, they argued, Americans have the right to choose not to buy health insurance. But Roberts ruled that not buying health insurance was itself an economic activity. We can now be punished not just for doing bad things, but for not doing things federal officials consider good.

Using the Supreme Court's logic, there is no such thing as a virgin because the process of deciding not to engage in sexual activity is itself a sexual activity.

17. QUALITY OF LIFE AND GRANITE COUNTERTOPS

MARK TWAIN HELPED POPULARIZE THE quip that "there are three kinds of lies: lies, damned lies, and statistics." The saying is even more apt today for a very good reason: people increasingly get their news and analysis from extremely biased sources.

When I first began teaching, almost all the students in my class shared the same general knowledge about current events in the world. While the students often arrived at different conclusions, at least they could engage in discussions based on similar facts.

About ten or so years ago, I realized my students were not obtaining their news analysis from sources similar to mine. By that time, the TV channel Comedy Central had apparently become the primary source of news analysis for many college students. In more recent years, the sources appear to have become a variety of cable news channels—all but one of which are quite leftist. Like most other people, students prefer to follow information sources that confirm their preferred beliefs. Leftist teachers and the internet are facilitating that bad habit.

It appears journalists are increasingly seeking to promote leftist messages regarding politics and economics. The plethora of economic statistics means each journalist can cherry-pick the statistic that best fits their desired message. If they do not like the political leadership, they can pick statistics that make it appear that the economy is in shambles, and vice versa. Bill Clinton was elected president in large part for campaigning that the economy was in bad shape: "It's the economy, stupid." But official statistics indicate that the recession ended more than a year prior to the 1992 election.

Take another example of a slanted use of statistics. Higher levels of national economic output allow societies to better meet their needs and desires. Over the last 35 years or more, the United States has been generally enjoying solid economic growth. So I was surprised a few years ago when students began claiming that the entire US economy had been in steady economic decline for several decades. Of course, I asked for proof. What I received was always the same: real median household income had been declining for many years. In other words, the students claimed that, adjusted for inflation, the mid-level American households were experiencing declining prosperity over the first dozen years of the 21st century.

I researched the matter. The first thing I found appeared to be a contradiction: real (inflation-adjusted) median *wages* were hitting an all-time high, but real median *household income* was languishing. How could wages be growing but household income be declining? There were several answers, especially that Americans were forming smaller and smaller households. As the number of people per household decreases, a household's total income decreases. But common sense indicates that, if the wages per person are increasing, economic opportunities are increasing.

A good sign of long-term economic growth is the type of house the average young family buys. I remember my parents' first house (after they finally managed to work their way out of living with my mother's parents for the first few years): a tiny ranch-style house with one bathroom, no dining room, and no garage. That was a typical suburban house in the 1950s. Today's young adults expect multiple bathrooms, garages, granite counters, elegant kitchens, gorgeous exteriors, etc. Yet these same students are convinced that the United States is in economic decline. Why do academics search for aberrant economic statistics to teach a message that is just not true?

In 2012, the median household income began to soar. Suddenly my students and liberal colleagues no longer wished to discuss that statistic. They turned their attention to other statistics and issues that seemed to support their new arguments of how awful America is. With over 4,000 economists on the federal payroll, there is no end to the number of statistics that can be conjured up to provide the illusion of new support for their false arguments.

18. MIND THE INEQUALITY GAP

WHEN I BEGAN TEACHING IN the early 1980s, income and wealth inequality were accepted by most of my students as facts of life. Those students were more interested in having good incomes than in rebelling against the system. In recent years many of my students enter my class viewing these inequalities as national shames that must be fixed quickly. They argue that everyone should have the right to a quality education, good health care, and a job with a salary that enables dignity.

To challenge them, I insist that a particular student give me their money or books. The student invariably refuses. I press the issue: why won't you? The student may argue that they need it. I ask whether they would concede if I found another student who had less money and a greater need. Eventually, the student cuts through the fluff and exclaims he or she will not give me their stuff because "It's mine."

This primes them for what comes next.

I point out that their support for rights to health care, education, and a job is tantamount to implying that government is the true owner of everyone's property. Further, a government authority should be able to force some people deemed to have too much stuff to help other people deemed to have too little stuff.

Our incredibly successful nation was founded on the concept of natural rights. Socialism denies the natural rights of its victims. I have witnessed decades of decline in student familiarity with the concept and importance of natural rights.

Natural rights are entitlements to life, liberty and the pursuit of happiness. More specifically, people have a right to their own bodies and the fruits of their own labor—along with whatever property they can get through trade based on mutual consent. There are no other rights in a truly free society. Students have been taught to believe in other rights, such as entitlements to stuff they need or want: a job with an attractive wage, quality health care and education, adequate food, etc. But enforcing these rights forces some people (people who produce more for society than they consume) to provide goods and services to other people (who consume more than they produce).

The rights to life, liberty and the pursuit of happiness are often termed natural rights; the rights to jobs, health care, and food are often termed claim rights. The distinction between the two types of rights centers on property rights. The view that property belongs to the people who created it using their own labor (and using stuff they obtained through exchange based on mutual consent) is a belief in private property rights. People who believe in private property rights tend to believe in natural rights. People who view property ownership as rightfully being assigned through a social process tend to believe in claim rights.

The students in my classes are not there to have fun. Finance is a tough subject. Unlike many of the "soft disciplines," only the top students get As in most finance courses. In the toughest part of the semester, I ask my students a simple question: If every student received the same job offers, compensation, and was guaranteed career longevity regardless of which major they took or what grades they received, how many would be in this class and be working hard? The simple truth is that few of the students would be there and none would be working hard to understand all of the material. Deep down they understand incentives and respond to them with self-interest but, on the surface, they express outrage over economic inequality.

In practice, people are often inconsistent. My students believe their money and their books are private property, but other people's property and money are not. In effect, they believe they have a right to liberty, but others don't.

19. The Fallacy of Dollar-Cost Averaging

I usually teach corporate finance because it is the "gateway course" to finance and because I enjoy introducing students to the discipline I love so much. But my specialty is investments.

Most people think smart, well-trained financial professionals make investments with better-than-average returns. But most financial scholars argue that achieving superior returns is challenging, and that few professionals can consistently generate higher investment returns through financial analysis.

One popular technique hyped as producing superior returns is dollar-cost averaging. The dollar-cost averaging strategy calls for making regular purchases of a particular stock or mutual fund by investing the same dollar amount each time period. For example, consider a stock trading with an average price of $20 per share in the last year and an investor willing to invest $1,000 each year in that stock. (Note that the number of shares the $1,000 will purchase will vary inversely with its price.) The motivation for the strategy is that more shares will be purchased when the price is low, say $15 (when 66.7 shares will be purchased), and fewer will be purchased when the price is high, say $25 (when only 40 shares will be purchased). Dollar-cost averaging supposedly enables lower average costs.

Let's look at an example to see how this strategy might work. Consider a stock that varies over a two-year period with one $1,000 purchase at $15 and one at $25. A total of 106.7 shares will be acquired for $2,000 at an average cost of $18.75. If the stock returns to the middle of its range ($20) the 106.7 shares will be worth $2,133—a 6.7 percent profit on a $2,000 investment in a stock that did not rise. It seems like dollar-cost averaging works nicely.

The fallacy of this investment strategy is that share prices trend (i.e., tend to move in a single direction) as often as they reverse (i.e., move back toward previous levels, or mean-revert). It is just as likely that the stock will go down to $5 per share or up to $35 per share as to return to $20 per share. So let's look at eight equally likely paths for the stock starting at $20 per share and experiencing price changes (up or down) of $5 in the first period, $10 in the second period, and $5 in the third period:

		Number of shares	Profit or Loss
1.	$20 =>$25 => $35 => $40	68.6	$743
2.	$20 =>$25 => $35 => $30	68.6	$57
3.	$20 =>$25 => $15 => $20	106.7	$133
4.	$20 =>$25 => $15 => $10	106.7	-$933
5.	$20 =>$15 => $25 => $30	106.7	$1200
6.	$20 =>$15 => $25 => $20	106.7	$133
7.	$20 =>$15 => $ 5 => $10	266.7	$667
8.	$20 =>$15 => $ 5 => $ 0	266.7	-$2000

Sadly, the net of the profits and losses over these eight outcomes is zero. The case for dollar-cost averaging assumes prices return to "normal" levels (scenarios 3 and 6, in which each produces $133 in profits) and therefore leaves out the disaster scenarios when they keep going down. Of course, if someone can predict when trending or reverting is more likely to occur, that is a different story. Beware of get-rich-quick schemes.

20. A FLOCK OF BIRDS AND A STOCK TRADER WALK INTO A BAR...

SINCE I TEACH FINANCE, QUITE a few of the students attracted to my course follow the stock market closely. They notice the extreme swings in individual stock prices and sometimes in the overall stock market. Often the swings in the overall stock market occur when there appears to have been little or no news to justify them. The students conclude, like many people, that these stock market extremes are caused primarily by emotions and irrationality.

But large price swings in well-developed financial markets are better viewed as natural, rational, and healthy. I believe this is true even if those swings are sometimes caused by trading itself.

Consider the price of the stock of a small oil firm. Its price will vary with shifting expectations of its ability to locate and tap supplies of crude oil. News of unsuccessful explorations will drive its stock price down, while news of successes will drive its price up. Given the erratic nature of news regarding the future of economic matters, we should expect that market prices of stocks should be large and erratic.

Stock prices change when good or bad news emerges. So we should expect traders to look at the stock price itself as a signal of whether the firm is experiencing success or failure in its efforts to earn profits. But, sometimes, stock prices move simply because of random trading. Perhaps more traders happen to be selling the stock to obtain cash than are buying the stock to deploy excess cash. It is difficult for a trader to know whether a recent price change was driven by random trading imbalances or news unknown to the trader. The trader faces the risk that he or she will mistakenly believe that a recent price drop comes from a temporary trading imbalance (that will soon reverse) when it might be the first wave of prolonged selling set in motion by bad news the trader has not heard.

The situation reminds me of the behavior of a flock of birds. I often observe perhaps fifty or so of them calmly searching for food in the grass. Then they all spring into the air, fly in a circle around the lawn, and return to the original spot. I believe this behavior is rational and healthy. Perhaps one of the birds saw a cat. Perhaps they mistook the shadow of a cloud as the shadow of a hawk. Perhaps two of the birds scared each other by inadvertently bumping into each other. The flock experiences a lot of false panics and a few real ones, and the birds have the common sense to know they are better off taking flight in either case.

The stock market experiences false panics as well. It is often said that stock prices "take the escalator up and the elevator down"—

indicating the tendency of stocks to slowly rise but quickly sell off. Sometimes the sell-offs are based on bad news—but often there is no apparent reason.

Many of the stock market sell-offs stem from traders' natural and healthy responses to the risks they face—just like the birds' taking flight is a perfectly rational response to their many sources of risk. The intelligentsia view these sell-offs as unnecessary. They try to control them with regulations, and they use them as reasons to insist market prices are irrational and should be replaced with valuations set by government committees. But we should respect both the birds and the stock traders. The birds are doing something we are unable to do: survive their entire lives in the wilderness. And the successful stock traders are doing something the elites cannot do: survive by consistently buying when stocks are underpriced and selling when stocks are overpriced.

Incidentally, although the news media tell us the opposite, the volatility of US stock market prices has been decreasing generally over the last 100+ years. Recent price volatility tends to be about half the volatility over the previous century. Perhaps markets are becoming even better at processing information efficiently and effectively.

21. THE ANIMAL FARM CALLED THE AMERICAN CAMPUS

THE INTELLIGENTSIA'S WAR AGAINST WESTERN civilization is founded on multiculturalism. The intelligentsia and political elitists are pushing our society toward the view that America desperately needs to embrace the values of all cultures and stop viewing Western values as preferable.

The primary goal of the cultural war is to debase everything associated with America. At the heart of this cultural war is a hoary and familiar objective: to transform this nation into a socialist utopia. The warriors' anthem is John Lennon's "Imagine," and their beliefs are as devoid of reason and empirical evidence as Lennon's song.

America's cultural war began in the 1960s with hatred for America's moral values and with a crusade by the intelligentsia to convince our society that sex should be free from traditional social norms, that LSD and other drugs are enlightening, and that communes are the ideal economic model. The elitists helped "free" American women of the burden of being respected if they chose to be a full-time mom.

Despite the failed outcomes from the cultural revolution of the '60s, American intelligentsia have maintained their arrogant belief that the nation should be guided by their superior knowledge.

If the multicultural revolution succeeds, the outcome will not be pretty. We see the evidence from examining those American jurisdictions and institutions where the intelligentsia and other progressive leftists have already won. America's major urban areas are disasters caused by centrally micromanaged school systems, bloated welfare rolls, and hostility to businesses. Judging from advertising in major urban areas, the only thriving businesses are law practices that seek clients to sue everyone for everything.

College and university campuses are a microcosm of the America to come if the multicultural revolution succeeds. Instead of becoming heterogeneous, open, and welcoming, the campuses have become homogeneous, exclusive, and hostile. Free speech has been driven out of most campuses.

The academic communities run by the intellectual elitists are not healthy. The victors on American campuses are fighting each other with quickly changing messages and alliances. The seething hatred and in-fighting under the surface of these communities stifle dissent and cast doubt on the communities' pretense to respect all as equals. Their absolute power leads to absolutely vicious in-fighting.

Events at Evergreen State College in Olympia, Washington provide a stunning example of liberals denying free speech—even to other liberals. At Evergreen, a liberal professor (Bret Weinstein) was threatened and forced off campus by lunatic leftists who were outraged when he challenged "a day of racial segregation" (See "When the Left Turns on Its Own" NY Times, 6/1/2017).

As George Orwell wrote, "All are equal, but some are more equal than others." Orwell wrote at the end of Animal Farm that the pigs became indistinguishable from the humans. In Orwell's remarkable story, humans were the previous leaders of the farm, while the pigs were the new leaders. At the book's end, Orwell described a meeting of the humans and pigs, noting that "twelve voices were shouting in anger, and they were all alike." The prospect for turmoil in America is even more frightening than the turmoil being observed on progressive campuses. Free speech is being shut down, and the progressive elites are becoming the establishment they despise.

22. COOPERATION AND COERCION: A DISTINCTION WITH A DIFFERENCE

COERCION HAS DELETERIOUS ECONOMIC CONSEQUENCES. But what does it really mean to coerce another person? What steps are involved? Many think the coercer must physically force the coerced person to do something against his or her will. When a parent says to a child, "Go to your bedroom and go to sleep," and the child responds, "I will not," the parent might pick the child up and carry him or her to bed. It is likely the child will fight every step of the way by squirming, screaming, and clutching onto doorframes. That is coercion.

But almost all coercion against adults isn't by physical force applied to their body—it's by the threat of violating their rights. Thus, there are usually two components: first, a threat, followed by the potential loss of a right of the person being coerced.

A threat without a potential loss of rights is not coercion. A threat to deny a person a privilege might be effective, but it is not coercion as the term is used in this book. If someone says to me, "Help me solve this problem, or I won't hire you as a consultant," they are attempting to cooperate with me, not to coerce me. But, if that person says to me, "Help me solve this problem, or I'll hit you and take your money," they are coercing me.

Agreement on the difference between cooperation and coercion requires agreement on the distinction between rights and privileges. Our society has slowly changed its view of rights. While the word "rights" used to mean the natural rights espoused by our Founding Fathers (life, liberty and the pursuit of happiness), now it is often interpreted as meaning the social rights espoused by the intelligentsia (jobs, health care, childcare, dignity).

The intelligentsia are wordsmiths. They take words for vile crimes such as rape and enslavement and apply them to issues involving no coercion or crime at all. They vilify businesspeople as slavers who rape people of their dignity by forcing them into low-paying jobs. But business people's "victims" voluntarily accept jobs offering low pay because it's the best opportunity they have. No one, including the elites, is willing to offer them a better opportunity. It seems as though the person offering another person an opportunity that is better than anything else anyone would offer them should be viewed as a hero, not a villain.

The word "slavery" is the proper word to describe the act of taking Africans from their homeland and separating families against their will. "Slavery" involves the use or threat of chaining, whipping, and beating. Americans accepting offers of low-paying jobs are not being coerced, and they are not being victimized by their new employers. Their rights are not being violated, and they are not being enslaved. They are accepting the best jobs anyone is willing to offer them. If someone thinks low-level workers are being robbed by being paid far less than they are worth, please step forward and open a business that offers them better terms of employment.

It has been said that the beginning of wisdom is calling things by their correct names. Let's discuss economics with clarity, not obfuscation.

23. ATTACKING THE FOUNDING FATHERS

MULTICULTURALISM IS A MOVEMENT CHAMPIONED by the intelligentsia and political elitists to degrade Western culture in general and American culture in particular, as being—at best—on par with all other cultures. In their minds, America deserves to be ashamed of its past and its present.

One of the newest fronts in the intelligentsia's war on American values is finding a real or perceived flaw in a white, non-liberal American male and using it to remove any vestige of respect for his legacy. To them, Lincoln was merely a political opportunist who had no compassion for slaves and who had no desire to end slavery. The elitists argue that all traces of respect for Jefferson's accomplishments should be rescinded because he was a slave owner and serial rapist. Our youth are being taught to hate America's Founding Fathers.

According to the political and academic elitists, America itself is and always has been a horrible nation: "White supremacy has been an organizing principle of American life since the founding of the

United States" (from an open letter signed by about 85 of my former colleagues after Trump's election). For more than two decades I have heard academic elitists rail against the United States while staying silent on the travesties—mostly against women and homosexuals—committed in other countries by such people as Che Guevara.

I treasure Martin Luther King, Jr.'s legacy of peace and compassion. It matters very little to me that this great man also had faults. For example, a committee of scholars appointed by Boston University found he had plagiarized passages in his dissertation for a doctoral degree there (*New York Times*, October 11, 1991). No one is perfect, and everyone has done shameful things that fly in the face of their true beliefs and lifetime of work. Each person should be evaluated on the totality of his or her service. And, on that basis, Martin Luther King, Jr. should be admired.

The evaluation of a person's life also needs to be made in the context of the times and society in which they lived. The naturalist John James Audubon loved birds and should be fully celebrated for his contributions to the study of birds, including his great artwork depicting many species. But apparently Audubon killed birds so he could use them more effectively as models for his artwork. This does not lower my opinion of Audubon. It simply deepens my understanding of the extent to which norms change and how the current norms of a society exert influence on the way we think and act.

Every cabinet member that ever served President John F. Kennedy was a white male. According to the dogma of the intelligentsia, this would make him a misogynistic racist. Yet there is no cry at Harvard and elsewhere to remove his name nor should there be. Times were different back then. Similarly, Jefferson, Lincoln, and King had courage and inspiration when they opened new frontiers, and they should be celebrated wholeheartedly.

The attacks on Jefferson, Lincoln, and others are not based on an agenda of opposing slavery. Thankfully, that war is over. The agenda is to discredit America's Founding Fathers in the intelligentsia's war to dismantle the natural rights that serve as the founding principles of the miracle known as America. The intelligentsia hate traditional American values. Their attack on prominent Americans is simply an effort to convert America into the multicultural paradise they envision.

24. WEALTH IS NOT A MIRAGE

YEARS AGO, I ATTENDED A conference at a luxury hotel attended by management professors from across the US. At a mealtime break, I joined a conversation and was quite surprised that the general theme was that the pursuit of personal or corporate wealth was evil. These professors were not just criticizing *overzealous* pursuit of wealth; they were criticizing any pursuit of wealth.

I was dumbfounded that these business school professors—people who devoted their professional lives to researching and teaching about wealth-seeking organizations—were so averse to the pursuit of wealth. I was also dumbfounded that they did not recognize the irony of staying at a luxury hotel while criticizing others for pursuing wealth.

So, if not pursuing wealth, what did they consider appropriate goals? It became apparent that they advocated pursuing high-quality health care and education, as well as pollution control, good nutrition, and high culture such as theater, art, and music. But how can a society achieve these outcomes without wealth? Of course, wealth facilitates these outcomes.

People with very little wealth struggle just to have enough food to eat. They cannot afford good health care and quality education. Throughout most centuries most people had so little wealth that they struggled just to survive. No matter how much they might wish to have quality health care and education, many people in the world's poorest societies must focus on the most important issue in their lives: obtaining enough food, clothing, and shelter to survive for the next few days.

As people attain higher levels of wealth, they can increasingly pursue goals beyond survival. Wealth is not a mirage—it is the foundation on which most of our individual and shared goals can be pursued.

25. And the Buyer and Seller Said, "Thank You" in Unison

John Stossel nicely captures the essence of the cooperation involved in trade by describing each trade as a "thank you-thank you" transaction. Both people must perceive that the trade is making them better off. Otherwise they would not agree to the trade. One person buys an item because the individual believes the money paid is worth less than the item received, while the other person believes the money received is worth more than the item delivered. When the trade is consummated, they each say, "Thank you."

The intelligentsia and political elitists have always had big problems with voluntary transactions. What if the price the two parties negotiate favors the wealthier one? The intelligentsia, who are mostly liberals, are not alone in condemning voluntary transactions: conservatives argue that trade should not be permitted if it involves sex or drugs. But libertarians argue that, if the two parties are consenting adults, then nobody has the right to block the transaction.

Academic economists have spawned a huge research program in support of placing the state's rights above the rights of the individuals involved in the thank you-thank you transactions. The centerpiece of their agenda is externalities. Economists note that virtually any human action directly or indirectly affects one or more individuals who are not parties to the transaction. Any such effect is termed an externality of the transaction. The actions of the buyer and seller exert positive and negative externalities on people who have no control over whether the transaction takes place. For example, if a restaurant hires a worker, taking him away from another employer, one negative externality might be the effect on that employer. A positive externality might be that the worker now can walk to his or her job, which could reduce traffic congestion and parking problems in the area.

Economists argue that governments must regulate or tax transactions with negative externalities. The poster child of the externality movement is pollution. Surely government must tax those who pollute or contribute to global warming. This is known as *pricing* the externalities.

A major problem with taxing people who cause externalities—or forcing them to compensate the people they harm—is that, in most cases, it is not clear how much harm was caused and what a reasonable value for that harm is. If my new restaurant causes traffic congestion, who should I compensate for their inconvenience, and what is a reasonable amount for the inconvenience?

Another huge problem with holding everyone accountable for negative externalities is opportunity costs. Economists agree that opportunity costs (the value foregone by not doing something) are as real as direct costs (the costs of doing something). So the argument for making people pay for the negative externalities caused by what they do implies that people should also pay for the opportunity costs (i.e., negative externalities) caused by what they do not do. When Michael Jordan left basketball for a stint in baseball, he harmed a lot of basketball fans who were denied the joy of watching him play. The loss of entertainment was a huge externality burdening people who had no say in the matter. Under the logic used by academic economists, Jordan should be held liable to compensate every basketball fan that suffered from his decision.

Our Founding Fathers provided a simple solution to the problem of externalities: resolving disputes based on preserving the natural rights of the parties involved. The whole point of rights is allowing people to pursue happiness, even when it harms other people, as long as the harm they cause does not violate other peoples' natural rights. Michael Jordan had a natural right to switch from basketball to baseball, no matter how much misery it caused basketball fans. Our society has lost sight of this key principle.

If the intelligentsia and political elitists succeed in restricting or taxing all actions causing negative externalities—even those that do not violate other people's natural rights—it will drive us toward a totalitarian society where the state dictates what everyone does and does not do to conform to what the leaders claim is optimal. That is exactly counter to the miraculous breakthrough the Founding Fathers made when they insisted that all people have a natural right to pursue their own happiness, limited only by the natural rights of others.

The geniuses who developed the concept of natural rights understood these very issues. They advocated establishing natural rights as safe harbors to protect people from the use of government to prevent people from pursuing their own happiness. Pollution can deny me the natural right to unpolluted air and water on my property. Therefore, government should make people accountable for causing harmful levels of pollution. I agree with most other economists on this particular issue. But, when someone decides not to date me, employ me, trade with me, or accommodate my disabilities, they may be hurting me, but they are not infringing on any natural right I possess. The alternative to a society based on natural rights is a society in which people must serve the whims of the powerful and, in doing so, make the powerful even more powerful.

26. WINS FOR LAWSUIT VICTIMS ARE LOSSES FOR CONSUMERS

HAVE YOU NOTICED THAT SOCIETY—ESPECIALLY our media—searches for people they can characterize as victims? On one side are lawyers advertising on billboards, TV, and the internet for people to see themselves as victims of disease, injury, or alleged injustice. On the other side are reporters, community organizers, and do-gooders searching for victims for whom they can conjure up sympathy and make the matter a problem that requires government intervention.

Teenagers and young adults are especially drawn to stories of perceived injustices. They celebrate when corporations are forced to pay out big bucks to a victim. It seems to fill some deep need they have to see the so-called privileged members of our society getting their just deserts.

But economic reasoning teaches us otherwise. Our overly litigious ways serve the rich much more than the poor. The costs of potential lawsuits—just like all other potential costs—are built into the prices businesses must charge. Students are outraged to hear that consumers ultimately pay most of the legal costs and damages associated with various products. But businesses have to include all of their expected costs in setting prices. Businesses do not really pay real estate taxes, income taxes, payroll taxes, and other taxes out of their profits. They build those costs—just like the costs of insurance, raw materials, labor, advertising and utilities—into the prices they charge. It is the consumers who pay for the expected costs of litigation. It should be equally clear that, when people shoplift from Walmart or any other store, it is the paying customers who suffer the loss. Stores must pass on their normal costs of doing business—and normal levels of theft and litigation are no exception to that principle. You and I are victims of these so-called victimless crimes.

Campuses are full of laments that women are victims because they are denied educational opportunities. However, approximately 60 percent of all bachelors' degrees in the United States are now awarded to women. Minority students have received preferential treatment in admissions to higher education for more than half a century. I have never heard these points celebrated or even mentioned on campus.

We have reached the point where people who fall, lose their jobs, or have a medical problem are almost guaranteed to be viewed by much of society as victims. The only question is: which successful person (or, better yet, which corporation) can be blamed and sued?

Victims who were harmed in large part by their own carelessness or by true accidents are not creating value or wealth when they and their lawyers file lawsuits seeking outrageous verdicts. They are using the coercion contained in our legal system to redistribute wealth. The time and energy of the lawyers, juries, judges, and so-called victims spent on needless litigation are losses to our society because they represent resources that were expended without creating any value. The more we go down that path, the smaller the pie becomes.

The juries and judges who are handing out the money to alleged victims are using other people's money. I have watched countless jurors brag on TV after another ridiculous verdict that they were happy to be able to give the plaintiffs a huge cash award. Of course, they did not give anybody anything; they forced someone who earned the money to pay it to someone who did not. The real people who are suffering financially and paying for the verdicts and fines are consumers: ordinary people who pay more every day for products and services because of the unjustified awards and other costs of a legal system run amok.

27. TAXING ROBOTS

BILL GATES DID A FEW things right, did a few things wrong, and speaks gibberish when he strays from his narrow range of expertise and tries to discuss economics.

Clearly, users of personal computers based on the IBM standard in the 1980s needed better software. Microsoft met that need. If it had not done so, some other firm would have. Many defenders of free markets try to argue that free markets produce results that are just. But Austrian economists avoid this trap. Markets often distribute massive rewards to people who do not appear to have made massive contributions. For example, recent social media ventures have spawned numerous billionaires in the last decade who just happened to be the first to market.

Bill Gates seems to think his intelligence matches his fortune. He often opines about solutions to the world's problems. In 2017, the *Financial Times* and other media reported that Gates wanted businesses to be taxed for using robots in the same way they are taxed for employing humans. Like many people, Gates apparently thinks all jobs are good jobs, even if they are unnecessary.

Why stop at using taxation to reduce the use of robots that threaten jobs? Why not destroy any equipment that does work that people could do? We could destroy printing presses and copiers to create jobs that pay people to serve as scribes. We could destroy all construction equipment to open up scads of jobs digging with shovels. What the heck, let's do as Milton Friedman sarcastically suggested—take away the shovels and give them spoons. Gates is not alone in opposing automation. Perennial doom-and-gloom and leftist economist Robert Shiller also supports taxing robots. Should agricultural equipment be taxed to the point that one out of every two Americans can joyfully return to the good old days of serving as manual laborers on farms?

If entrepreneurs are free to implement new ideas for meeting the needs and wants of the entire population, there will always be employment available. We need to eliminate taxes on wages and repeal minimum-wage legislation. We need to innovate to destroy every job that can be done more efficiently by machines in order to free up labor for jobs that cannot be done by machines.

The key to prosperity—which has provided people today with incredible opportunities—is to use humans as productively as possible. Continued growth in economic opportunities depends on the continued destruction of every job that can be made unnecessary through advances in technology.

Progress requires getting rid of old, inefficient methods. In this process, people lose old jobs and move to new jobs. We have full employment today—although most of the jobs today did not exist a century ago. Change can be painful—but not as painful as being in an economy with no growth where everyone is stuck in the past.

Some people—elitists—lament that the increased wealth from economic growth accrues primarily to the wealthy. What is the verdict for free markets that produce unjust outcomes? To apply Winston Churchill's quote on democracy: "Free markets are the worst economic system, except for all the others." History is replete with proof that every other economic system pales in comparison with the incredible success of America's free markets. The American economic system paved the way for the incredible advances the entire world increasingly enjoys. If we listen to the elites, including Bill Gates and

Robert Shiller, we will suffer in the long run as others advance while we regress into poverty.

28. CHESS LESSONS

AS A YOUTH, I COMPETED frequently in chess tournaments and witnessed first-hand the incredible skill that people develop when they focus their energies on a task. Throughout history, chess enthusiasts have developed chess openings—sequences of initial moves—that would give them advantages. Many of the most well-known chess openings are named after their originators.

The sophistication of tournament chess has improved through the years due to the accumulated knowledge of successful openings and strategies, just like economic efficiency has increased through the accumulated knowledge of better production methods.

In both cases, there need not be a mastermind micromanaging the process of innovation or a government body orchestrating the adoption of new ideas. In chess, nobody votes that a particular innovation needs to be used by anyone else or can't be used by anyone else. There are no departments or agencies that need to spend government money to subsidize innovations, regulate change, or levy taxes. It is simply self-interest at work in a competitive market.

In the case of chess, the value of a new opening becomes known when its originator uses it successfully in a tournament. When confronted with the success of a new opening introduced by its originator, other chess players study the new opening, experiment with potential counters to that opening, and, sometimes, improve the original opening or construct a defense that renders it obsolete. The best openings persist and evolve, with new ideas that are tested in tournaments and continually revised in a back-and-forth battle between the innovations that emerge on both the offensive and defensive sides of the opening.

A free market economy works the same way. Competition continuously drives market participants to search for better production and distribution methods—methods that lower costs or improve performance. In free markets, the best competitors tend to win the prize of greater market share. But there is another way to succeed when government is corrupt: prevent others from being allowed to compete against you.

In political discussions, there is a similar way to succeed: prevent others from participating in public discourse if they disagree with the intelligentsia. Label those who disagree with the elites as bigots and racists. Describe their ideas as hate speech and make it illegal. And, most effective of all in the long run, take control of a country's educational system and silence all voices that compete against leftist ideologies. Checkmate.

29. THE EHRLICH-SIMON BET

PRESIDENT JIMMY CARTER VIEWED THE US economy as fragile, free markets as unable to solve major problems, and increased federal control of the economy as the solution. Many people seem to have an inordinate fear that, in a free market, there will be serious shortages. They wonder how there can be enough food, raw materials, or energy products for the future if our federal government is not heavily involved in making sure it happens. They don't seem to notice that the vast majority of shortages occur in centrally planned economies.

In 1924, Ira Joralemon warned, "The age of electricity and of copper will be short. At the intense rate of production that must come, the copper supply of the world will last hardly a score of years.... Our civilization based on electrical power will dwindle and die."

Joralemon was not a quack; he was a Harvard graduate, a geologist, and arguably the foremost copper-mining expert in the world at the time of this prediction. His warning was tantamount to a "peak" copper warning—a type of warning about diminishing resources that is now commonplace.

Joralemon is not the only credentialed person who has made big mistakes in trying to predict economic outcomes. Experts have warned of dire shortages for years. Paul Ehrlich, a Stanford University biology professor, became well known with the publication of his controversial 1968 book, *The Population Bomb*. The original version began with this statement: "The battle to feed all of humanity is over. In the 1970s hundreds of millions of people will starve to death in spite of any crash programs embarked upon now. At this late date, nothing can prevent a substantial increase in the world death rate." Ehrlich not only predicted mass famines, he also predicted huge shortages of important commodities because he could not imagine how the world could meet the needs of its growing population.

Julian L. Simon, a business professor at the University of Maryland, disagreed with Ehrlich's doom-and-gloom forecasts. He understood the ability of humans to innovate. He entered into a famous ten-year wager with Ehrlich in 1980. Ehrlich was allowed to choose five commodity metals he believed would rise in price over the next ten years due to increased population. Ehrlich, with the aid of the experts he consulted, picked these five metals: copper, chromium, nickel, tin, and tungsten. Ehrlich lost the bet: the inflation-adjusted prices of all five commodities trended downward during the ten-year wager period. In 1990, Ehrlich paid Simon to settle the wager.

But arrogant so-called experts such as Ehrlich are seldom in doubt, despite being frequently wrong. On December 2, 1990, Paul Ehrlich declared, "The bet doesn't mean anything" ("Betting on the Planet,"

New York Times Magazine, December 2, 1990).

You would think Ehrlich's poor record of predictions would lead him to keep his predictions to himself or rethink his beliefs. But, recently, Paul Ehrlich has been back on the fear-mongering wagon with an especially ignorant treatise on how society must "mend societal fundamentals," the centerpiece of which is a proposal to cap the income of the extremely wealthy.

The key to the fallacy of peak oil or peak anything else is that the predictor presumes they can understand the limits on the future ability of the world's billions of people to develop new technologies and to respond to changing conditions. Almost by definition, predicting advances in technology is nearly impossible. I remember reading *Popular Science* and *Popular Mechanics* magazines fifty years ago as a child and being fascinated by their predictions that we would soon live in a world of easy-to-use jetpacks and personal helicopters—which has not come close to happening. Conversely, I do not remember reading any predictions in those magazines about an innovation that would allow widespread, wireless, and instant access to vast amounts of information.

It is difficult to predict the future, but our youth have been indoctrinated by these fear mongers with a decidedly anti-Western prophecy of doom. Our youth will eventually come to understand that, generally, such fear mongers are not focused on unbiased examination of the evidence. They are not evidence-based. In fact, most of us are very poor scientists. But, in my experience, the intelligentsia are the worst scientists, because they believe mostly those things they wished were true. And, make no mistake about it, the intelligentsia want economic freedom to fail so that America will anoint them with the power to manage the economy.

30. FDR's Second Bill of Rights

SOME AMERICANS ARE RIGHTFULLY CONCERNED that socialism has been secretly infiltrating our culture. Credit must be given to President Franklin D. Roosevelt for being transparent and honest about the matter. In a national radio address on January 11, 1944, FDR proposed a second bill of rights. Here is the critical part:

To assure us equality in the pursuit of happiness... economic truths have become accepted as self-evident. We have accepted, so to speak, a second Bill of Rights.... Among these are:

- The right to a useful and remunerative job;
- The right to earn enough to provide adequate food and clothing and recreation;
- The right of every farmer to raise and sell his products at a return which will give him and his family a decent living;
- The right of every businessman, large and small, to trade in an atmosphere of freedom from unfair competition and domination by monopolies at home or abroad;
- The right of every family to a decent home;
- The right to adequate medical care and the opportunity to achieve and enjoy good health;
- The right to adequate protection from the economic fears of old age, sickness, accident, and unemployment;
- The right to a good education

FDR claimed that these rights had become accepted in America and that it was time to strengthen and formalize them as the foundation for a peaceful and just society. But many of these rights are the foundations of socialism—for example, the "right to a useful and remunerative job." Defining that right implies that someone has to provide the job and that someone else decides what is useful and what constitutes "remunerative." Both implications mean government coercion must be used to force people to provide jobs they don't want to provide. Likewise, socialistic rights mean that people must buy products they don't want and must pay higher prices than they would otherwise pay. Exercising this coercion requires central planners to weigh the myriad benefits and costs involved. But, with government distorting market prices, society no longer has reliable market data with which to weigh the true benefits and costs in a world of rapidly changing technology and conditions.

FDR's listed rights were not all socialistic. Perhaps the most frightening proposals were the rights that serve as foundations of crony capitalism—the partnerships between business and government that erode economic freedoms. Examples of these so-called rights include that farms should be able to produce what they want and still receive a fair rate of return, and that businesses should not face "unfair" competition. Why might these crony capitalist rights be worse than the socialistic rights? Because they allow influential business owners and farmers to gain unnatural economic control over the rest of us.

Some of my students find some of FDR's proposals attractive. Why can't we impose a few rules so that people who are struggling can make a decent living? Because it's like nurturing cancer. These kinds of regulations favor lousy business models and methods and help them metastasize. For the most part, when a businessperson or farmer weighs benefits and costs poorly, they lose money and, if they persist in poor decision-making, they destroy their businesses or lose their farms or businesses. In a free market, business practices that destroy wealth perish and those that create value take their place. The alternative is much more painful; just ask the Venezuelans. Effective cancer treatment involves destroying the bad cells just like free competition destroys bad businesses—both of which are healthy outcomes.

31. THE CORRUPTION OF ROBIN HOOD

THERE ARE TWO COMPETING INTERPRETATIONS of the story of Robin Hood. Many people describe Robin Hood as a legendary Englishman who stole from the rich and gave to the poor. Others recall that the story was a little more complicated. In their story, Robin Hood took money from tax collectors and unscrupulous landowners and returned it to the people from whom they'd stolen it.

There is a big difference between these versions. The "stealing from the rich and giving to the poor" version suggests that we should admire Robin Hood because poor people are entitled to money held by rich people; therefore, what he did should be viewed as justice, not stealing. The alternative version tells us to admire Robin Hood for risking his life to return money a corrupt government had unjustly taken away.

Progress in society comes from advances made by individuals. For humankind to excel, we need to let functional activities be rewarded and dysfunctional activities be punished. The economic influence of value creators needs to rise, and the economic influence of wealth destroyers must decline. We all benefit from an economic system that promotes constructive behavior and discourages destructive behavior.

I have no problem with a functional guy named Peter deciding to give some of his earnings to a dysfunctional guy named Paul. Perhaps Peter knows Paul and knows that Paul is working to correct his dysfunctions, or perhaps he knows that Paul has no control over his dysfunctions. Regardless, it is Peter's money, and therefore it is Peter's decision.

My problem is when a guy named Pat forces a functional person such as Peter to give his earnings to a dysfunctional Paul. For starters, I fear that Pat might have little motivation to ensure the money is well spent because it is not his money. Worse, I fear Pat is trying to curry favor with Paul so that both Pat and Paul can vote to take more money from Peter. Today, people increasingly see Paul as a victim rather than a freeloader. Many people see him more as the hero and the source of society's wealth, and Peter as the one percent of society who freeloads off the hardworking 99 percent.

Society can be likened to a garden. My wife is a gifted gardener. When she sees a plant with a few bad leaves, she tears off the leaves. I used to view this as damaging the plant. But she knows that proper pruning guides the plant to use its energies elsewhere. When a plant fails to thrive, she digs it up and starts over with a new plant. It is tough to argue with her methods because, year after year, her gardens thrive.

Of course, I don't believe people, no matter how dysfunctional, should be uprooted or otherwise physically harmed because they are dysfunctional. But the progress of humankind requires processes that discourage people's dysfunctional behaviors by causing those people to bear the negative consequences of those behaviors. Progress also requires that creators of value be protected from those who would steal it.

32. TRULY FREE SPEECH HURTS

MY STUDENTS ARE SHOCKED WHEN I tell them I believe that, in one way, we benefit from the actions of the Westboro Baptist Church when they picket military funerals. Of course, I disdain their message that God is allowing soldiers to be killed as punishment for America's support for gay rights. But a significant benefit of their actions is that those actions raise the question of whether Americans genuinely have the right to freedom of speech. That our government protects them sends the message that free people are protected, no matter how unpopular their opinions, as long as they are not infringing on the natural rights of others.

Not all debates regarding our freedoms are easy to resolve. Noise pollution is an example. Two things are apparent: people must have the right to make some noise, and people must have the right to be protected from deafening noises. There are legitimate debates about the lines that must be drawn in resolving conflicting rights.

We must acknowledge that virtually everything we do can conceivably be seen as violating the rights of others. Some might cogently argue that a utility company should not have the right to spew carbon dioxide into the air because it may cause environmental damage. But this argument cannot be universally applied. Humans emit carbon dioxide when they breathe, so emitting carbon dioxide through breathing is linked to the natural right to life.

Another issue arises when the natural rights of two people conflict. One of the most famous economic principles on this issue is the Coase theorem, originated by renowned economist and Nobel laureate Ronald Coase. He proposed an example of a train throwing out sparks while passing by a wheat field. Does the train company have the right to throw out sparks, or does the farmer have the right to grow wheat next to the railroad tracks? Coase argued that markets allow for an efficient resolution to the dispute, no matter whose side wins any legal decision (i.e., no matter whom the law assigns the rights to).

Modern economies are filled with legitimate conflicts over rights. But the debate about American economic policies has strayed so far to the left that many discussions have become one-sided:

- Businesses should be forced to pay equal wages for work the government views as equal.

- Fast-food restaurants should be forced to offer healthy food choices.

- Government should set a high minimum wage and force taxpayers to pay "prevailing wages" on government-funded projects.

When I applied for and was accepted for my first job at a McDonald's restaurant in Riverside, New York, I agreed to work for $1.65 per hour. McDonald's did not enslave me. I loved working there. I received excellent training, and I learned valuable lessons that have benefited me throughout my entire life.

People who apply for jobs, accept the posts, and continue to show up to work each day are not enslaved. They are pursuing the best opportunity they can find. Employers like Walmart and McDonald's are not abusing their employees. They are offering their employees better opportunities than anyone else is offering them. If activists want the poor to do better than working at Walmart and McDonald's, they should go out and start their own businesses and use their own money to offer better jobs.

I still have the crude nametag I received when I began my job at McDonald's more than forty years ago. Above my name, it reads: *"May I help you?"* Commerce is about people helping each other voluntarily. The political elitists fantasize about utopian societies with centralized control over all economic matters, but the actual experiences with authoritarianism throughout the world reveal the truth: authoritarian regimes oppress the common man and woman. The intellectual elite argue that we just haven't implemented communism and other authoritarian regimes with the right leaders. Clear thinking tells us that no leader restricting liberty will ever be able to successfully micromanage a large, modern economy for an extended period.

33. HATE, AMERICAN STYLE

DO THE INTELLIGENTSIA AND POLITICAL elitists really hate America? I believe they hate America's past and present. And the hatred of progressive leftists for America is especially strident for anything related to America's productivity, wealth, or income. If America trades with a smaller country, the left characterizes it as exploitation. If America boycotts trade with another country, it is vindictive, arrogant, and cruel. If America trades with a large country, it is destructive globalization.

When elitists claim to love America, they are referring to their vision of what America could become in the future under their leadership (a politically correct socialist utopia). Their only fond feelings for America's history are for those Americans who opposed traditional American values. Their hearts tend to be with Europe's socialist nations, and their sympathies are with countries such as Cuba that have leaders that hate America. This sounds harsh, but it is the reality.

The intelligentsia hate America's economic values so much that they will overlook vital social issues. In all my years on various campuses, I have never seen or heard a public rebuke by the faculty of the atrocities committed by other nations against their own women, children, and homosexuals. Never. The list of atrocities is heartbreaking: stoning, mutilation, genocide, denial of education to girls, failure to prosecute rapes, laws denying women rights such as driving, etc. But leftists on American campuses consider a discussion of these issues an attack on non-Western societies, so it doesn't happen. The political elitists are focused on the victims of America's so-called predatory policies. The only criticisms allowed by the intelligentsia on campuses are attacks on Western values and people who support those values.

In all my years on various campuses, I have never seen or heard public praise for America's contributions over the last century, such as defeating dictatorships in WWII. American soldiers died for others while not taking possession of the territories on which those lives were lost, and the US provided massive amounts of foreign aid, bore disproportionate financial burdens for the UN and NATO, and more.

I have never heard an economist attack OPEC nations for their overt collusion in reducing oil production and raising oil prices. But I have heard economists attack the American pharmaceutical industry for not doing enough to help poor countries, even though they already provide medicine at much lower prices to those nations than they charge for the same medication sold in America.

The intelligentsia's hatred for America as it exists today runs deep and wide.

34. FEEDING THE WELFARE MONSTER

TRILLIONS OF DOLLARS HAVE BEEN thrown into America's social programs, starting during the Great Depression and accelerating into the 21st century, with little to show for it. The programs' failures were evident enough more than 50 years ago in 1964, when Ronald Reagan argued in a speech:

"So they are going to solve all the problems of human misery through government and government planning. Well, now, if government planning and welfare had the answer and they've had almost 30 years of it, shouldn't we expect government to almost read the score to us once in a while? Shouldn't they be telling us about the decline each year in the number of people needing help? The reduction in need for public housing? But the reverse is true. Each year the need grows greater, the program grows greater."

The 50 years since Reagan delivered that speech have seen broader and more extensive welfare programs. The net result is more and more economically dysfunctional people. When we reward the dysfunctional by taking money from the functional, we are inverting the natural forces that discourage dysfunction.

I often ask my students whether they enter a debate hoping to win or hoping to lose. As I grow older, I find myself increasingly eager to learn new things, and, therefore, I am becoming much more willing to learn while losing debates. I would like to lose the debate about welfare. I truly wish I were wrong and that someone could show me the problems of America could be solved by continuing in the direction our government has been headed. It would certainly be easier than to believe, as I do, that the solution is to let natural forces punish dysfunctional behaviors so that people on dysfunctional paths are naturally incentivized to make healthful changes in their lives.

35. PUBLIC SERVANTS

HIGH-LEVEL GOVERNMENT EMPLOYEES REFER TO themselves as public servants, but nothing could be further from the truth. These so-called public servants, in fact, serve as masters, deciding how much of our earnings we can keep and what we can and cannot do with our property. High-level "public servants" are increasingly the new royalty.

Even lower-level government employees act as part of a master class. I don't remember ever seeing a police car substantially exceeding the speed limit when I was young unless it had its emergency lights flashing. It surely was not common where I grew up in upstate New York. The only reasonable excuse a government official had for breaking traffic laws was if there was a need for a prompt response.

Speed ahead a half-century to today. I can't remember the last time I saw a police car—with or without emergency lights on—traveling at or below the speed limit. Normally, a police car whips down the passing lane only to pull over and set a speed trap. On what moral or legal basis can they disregard the rules of the road?

A few years ago, John Corzine, governor of New Jersey at the time, rode in an SUV from a conference to a scheduled event. A state trooper drove the SUV more than 90 miles per hour and used its emergency lights.

This was not an emergency; a report concluded that the trooper's use of emergency lights was unauthorized. In fact, the use of the emergency lights contributed to an accident. Two pickup trucks in front of the SUV saw the emergency lights and collided while swerving to get out of its way. We only know these "public servants" acted above the law because a horrible crash ensued. Surely there are far more instances that don't make headlines.

Equally telling is that Corzine was not wearing a seatbelt, even as the government he oversees mandates that ordinary citizens wear them.

This nation began with a radical vision of a government of the people, by the people, and for the people. Yet we seem to be turning into a country where government officials, from SWAT teams to politicians, are above the law.

36. THE RIGHT TO HARM OTHERS

IN THE LAST CENTURY, THERE has been a monumental shift: we now declare that people have economic rights that previously were seen as mere privileges. We absolve workers and consumers of individual responsibility, pamper them with protections, and offer them opportunities to seek jury awards for astounding amounts of money. Billboards and TV commercials troll for people who might have suffered from side effects of medicine made by manufacturers with deep pockets.

Nowadays, the idea that someone has been harmed is accepted as proof that they have been wronged and that any entity that contributed to the harm should be held liable. It is a grave mistake to think that, just because someone was harmed by another person, the other person must have done something morally and legally wrong and the law should rectify the harm.

Almost every action we take in the marketplace hurts other people. If I don't buy a product from XYZ Corporation, it hurts XYZ's employees and owners. If I do purchase something from XYZ, then I am hurting the employees and owners of XYZ's competitors.

Think about the harm Jane causes to others if she opens a new and successful restaurant:

- Other restaurants are likely to lose customers to the new restaurant.

- The employees Jane hires might quit their previous jobs, causing harm to their former employers.

- Traffic near Jane's restaurant will become more congested, and parking will be harder to come by.

- Some customers might overeat and develop health problems.

- Other entrepreneurs might lose the opportunity to open a similar restaurant first.

The list of potentially harmed people is long, and the grievances can be serious. Natural rights protect Jane from opening the restaurant, even if doing so harms others and even if it doesn't end up benefiting anyone much. In general, natural rights allow society to flourish.

One of the key measures of the economic liberty of a nation is whether the ordinary citizen can start his or her own business—and how much time and government fees it takes to do so. New, small businesses are the seeds of economic prosperity, and economic prosperity is the foundation of a healthy, well-educated, safe society. But there are many special interests that want to stop new firms from entering the marketplace. These special interests can find tons of potential harm that new firms might cause, and these special interests are increasingly winning in their efforts to halt economic change. Anybody that Jane's restaurant might harm can find ways to thwart her entrepreneurial venture. This is a form of crony capitalism. Our only hope is to reaffirm this nation's founding beliefs in a system of natural rights and responsibilities, rather than a system run by special interests.

37. FISHING FOR A HEALTHIER ENVIRONMENT

ENVIRONMENTAL PROTECTION IS A HOT topic on college campuses— and free enterprise is often depicted as the environment's number one enemy. But, when I was in Poland, I witnessed massive environmental damage in the portions of the country that were heirs of the era of Soviet domination. When private property became public property, people lost their incentive to protect the property.

I invited a prominent economist to campus one year who specialized in environmental protection. She led a fascinating exercise that simulated fishing the ocean by offering students an opportunity to make some quick cash playing an easy game. She invited students to volunteer as fishers. She positioned the students in a circle as she described the rules. Each student was given opportunities to "catch" as many small, gold-colored, fish-shaped crackers as they could, subject to the rules of the game.

The economist explained that, at the end of each game, each student would be rewarded with real cash based on how many crackers they caught. After each of several rounds of the game, the amount of cash the students received per fish would go up. She paid higher rewards in later rounds to simulate the real world—if the fish were not caught in the early rounds, they would have an opportunity to grow and reproduce. She threw a handful of the crackers on the floor and gave the signal to start fishing. The students dropped and gathered up all the fish in about three seconds.

She asked the students why they caught all the fish when she had told them the amount of money they could get would go up if they waited to catch the fish until another round. Their answer was simple: If they hadn't caught the fish, someone else would have.

She then changed the rules. She divided the space on the floor into one region for each student. Each student could only catch fish in their region. This time most, if not all, of the students decided to leave the fish in their region in the first round. Most students now realized they could be patient in catching the fish because the dividers between regions protected the fish from the other students.

She then led the students in a discussion of what this lesson taught them about protecting the environment. The students got it. When people own property, they tend to take care of it. When everybody owns it, nobody takes care of it. She went on to discuss the many failed ways government has tried to prevent overfishing in the ocean by limiting the number of boats, which motivated the fishers to buy bigger boats, and by limiting the length of each boat, which led the fishers to make wider boats, etc.

The economic principle she taught was the tragedy of the commons. Whenever people communally own property, they exploit it without regard for the long-term consequences. The reason is quite simple: each person can reap considerable short-term benefits from damaging the property (as with overfishing the ocean) but lose little because the long-term losses are split among all of them. That is one important reason why clear private property rights are a key to pursuing the joint goals of economic growth and environmental protection. Wealthy societies can afford to protect their environments, and it is private property rights that motivate them to do so.

38. BORN INTO COMMUNISM

I AM ORIGINALLY FROM UPSTATE New York, where I was born and raised in a commune. All the commune members were given food and other items based on our perceived needs. We were assigned duties based on our perceived abilities. I had little or no freedom to produce and consume what I wanted.

Actually, most of us share this history. We were almost all born and raised on communes. Most Americans were raised in the communal arrangement more commonly described as the typical American family. And these communes are not the voluntary and democratic hippie communes of the 1960s. As much as I like the concept of traditional families, the traditional family unit is not just a commune; it is a coercive and authoritarian regime. I'm not attacking the family unit; I'm simply recognizing it for what it is.

Survival as an infant requires some degree of socialism and coercion. Children can't produce the resources necessary for their survival. Others must give them food and other resources. Children don't have the judgment necessary to thrive. Children depend on a central authority (usually parents) to not only provide instruction but to apply coercion when necessary. What child hasn't, at some point, been forcefully prevented from running into the path of a car, stepping off a high ledge, or wandering into some other dangerous situation?

In these small family groups, children learn that central planning, autocratic leadership, and coercion are necessary for most endeavors. Imagine a household in which parents don't provide guidance and enforce no rules. I wouldn't have survived long in such a household. As it was, I tried to climb a ladder when I was 14 months old and ended up breaking my arm. I definitely needed coercion. My mother often said, "If Donnie had been my first child, he would have been my only child."

The concept of communal living and the use of coercion are not limited to family life. Most kids are forced to go to schools where teachers regularly promote socialist living. They proclaim the importance of sharing and equity. They typically enforce the doctrine that items such as snacks brought from home must be shared with the entire class and that the entire class must be punished for the actions of the few.

Many of the lessons we learned as children regarding communal arrangements are useful in adult life. We learned to coexist with roommates, housemates, friends, spouses, and our own children. But adults don't benefit from being coerced like children. Some lessons learned early in life about socialist arrangements and the use of coercion provide an inadequate framework for understanding how to thrive in adulthood, especially in large groups. Forcing other adults to behave the way we want when they're not hurting anyone but themselves is a knee-jerk reaction we need to reconsider. The nanny state treats adults like children. Adults should treat other adults like adults.

39. FREE OF TRADE

I OFTEN ASK ECONOMICS PROFESSORS what would happen to a societ if it permanently abolished all trade. They always answer that societ would suffer a rapid, one-time loss in productivity, but the size of tha loss would not be catastrophic and the effects would not be lasting.

I believe the correct answer is that virtually all people would di within a few years. With all trade abolished, all people would have t provide all their own food and water. Everyone would be forced to liv near a year-round water supply because no one could buy water from someone else or buy the equipment with which to transport water Rivers and lakes would become magnets for hordes of people. These congested areas would be rapidly depleted of food. These congested areas would become breeding grounds for diseases, causing massive outbreaks for which there would be no modern medicine once people consumed the existing stocks of medicines. After all, how could any single person—or rather, every single person—produce modern medicine such as antibiotics with their labor alone? And, without adequate game to hunt or equipment to farm, very few, if any, could feed themselves.

But what if there was enough clean water and game animals tha some people could survive in isolation from the urban masses for a least some time? Take Christopher McCandless, a bright young college graduate who attempted to survive alone in the Alaskan wilderness during the summer of 1992. His story was popularized by a book and movie titled, *Into the Wild*. McCandless brought with him numerous goods he had obtained through exchange: a gun, ammunition, clothing, food, and survival literature. In the wilderness, he found an abandoned bus with a stove that had apparently been used by others as a hunting cabin. Despite all these resources and being surrounded by

ame animals, McCandless died of malnutrition in approximately four months, weighing 66 pounds. He realized he was starving to death but was unable to return to civilization because a river's rising waters had trapped him. Virtually all of us would die at least this quickly if we were no longer able to exchange with one another.

The reason economists have such difficulty seeing the importance of exchange for survival is that they are trained to analyze economic activity on a marginal basis, viewing each action for its incremental benefits and costs. They see what would happen with fewer exchanges, but not with none at all. The marginal approach that economists use is indeed useful, but it leads many academics to underestimate the importance of trade.

Many academics advocate strong government controls to discourage trade, including heavy taxation and regulation. Our society is so anti-commerce that it taxes labor we provide to others while not taxing labor we provide for ourselves. For example, labor provided for one's own benefit (such as cleaning one's house) is not taxed, but labor provided for others (such as cleaning other people's houses) is regulated and heavily taxed. It makes no sense to punish goods and services provided to others because it is through exchanging our goods and services that we get the economic efficiencies that allow society to advance.

President Ronald Reagan famously pointed to the problem: "Government's view of the economy could be summed up in a few short phrases: If it moves, tax it. If it keeps moving, regulate it. And if it stops moving, subsidize it."

40. THE POWER OF THE FUTURE

PEOPLE IN THEIR TWENTIES HAVE been raised to believe there is only one reasonable source of power (electricity) and only one appropriate way to generate that power (solar). It is a cultish belief. Anyone disagreeing with this mantra gets branded a Jurassic-era, global-warming-denying hate monger. Here is how electricity has been generated recently in the United States:

Coal:	33.0%
Natural gas:	33.0%
Nuclear:	20.0%
Hydropower:	6.0%
Wind:	4.7%
Biomass:	1.6%
Petroleum:	1.0%
Solar:	1.0%

Let's view this list from the perspective of the intelligentsia and political elitists. Coal, natural gas and petroleum—hydrocarbons—are clearly and quickly destroying the planet. Nuclear energy destroys the planet through its radioactive waste and inevitable apocalyptic meltdowns. Hydropower destroys rivers and wildlife. Wind power kills birds and is "ugly." Biomass harms the environment and raises the price of food. But solar is the energy of the future.

My only success with communicating the pipedream-like nature of solar power in class is when I play a video of President Jimmy Carter from 1979. That summer, President Carter delivered the famous "malaise" speech when inflation was near its peak, and the nation appeared to be slipping further and further into a mess of poor economic performance, energy crises, and diplomatic disgrace. Carter claimed the problems facing the nation could only be solved if it overcame its "crisis of confidence." Although he never used the word "malaise," it's tough not to get a feeling of debility just from watching the speech. While Reagan would come along and portray expansive and wasteful government as the problem, Carter proposed that, to overcome our crisis of confidence, we needed to assess higher taxes, fork over increased subsidies, regulate more behavior, and even ration goods and services. In his "malaise speech," Carter vowed:

"I will soon submit legislation to Congress calling for the creation of this Nation's first solar bank, which will help us achieve the crucial goal of 20 percent of our energy coming from solar power by the year 2000. These efforts will cost money, a lot of money, and that is why Congress must enact the windfall profits tax without delay. It will be money well spent."

What most attracts the attention of my students is Carter's call for government to invest in solar-powered electricity because it demonstrates that federal government subsidization of solar power is not new. The impact of this video on today's college students can be dramatic. Here is Democrat Jimmy Carter, a Nobel laureate and maker of homes for the poor, preaching the gospel of solar power forty years ago—more than twenty years before my students were born. And, instead of reaching the goal of twenty percent solar in twenty years, we have achieved one percent in 40 years.

This reminds me of the famous TV show *Shark Tank*. On that show, aspiring entrepreneurs seek money from five venture capital investors. *Shark Tank* illustrates the world of venture capital quite well. It depicts venture capitalists eager to find projects whose benefits significantly exceed their costs. Some entrepreneurs receive pledges of capital from the investors, while others fail to secure funding for their ideas. The rejected entrepreneurs leave the stage and walk down a hallway, presumably contemplating how to cope with the bad news.

A more realistic version of *Shark Tank* would have the entrepreneur walk down the hallway to a desk where a government official sits. The government official would then decide whether to use the taxpayer's checkbook to fund the project even though no venture capitalist wanted to. Why should taxpayers fund such projects? Why should we believe government officials are better able to evaluate opportunities than people with their own money on the line?

Consider the solar-energy firm Solyndra. In 2009, Solyndra received a US Energy Department loan guarantee for $536 million as the first beneficiary of President Obama's stimulus program under the American Recovery and Reinvestment Act. Further, Solyndra received a $25 million tax break from the state of California. The loan guarantee meant Solyndra had cheaper access to capital. The tax break, not available to its competitors, was just like an outright subsidy. Despite all of this largesse at taxpayer expense, Solyndra declared bankruptcy, and the federal government received nothing.

In his speech, Carter raged against Americans who pursued their self-interests, insisting that self-interest was the problem and could never be a solution. But, about thirty years later, America vastly increased energy production through advances in the extraction of oil and gas. And the sources of those advances were small firms trying to make a profit by becoming more efficient using more effective technologies. Carter underestimated the ability of Americans to solve the problems they faced if given the freedom to do so. Like many politicians, Carter was frequently wrong, but never in doubt.

The intelligentsia and political elitists have it right; solar is the power of the future. It always has been, and it will be for some time to come. The current problem with solar power is not generating it; the problem is storing it. Solar power will not become the dominant source of American electricity until batteries or some other storage device holds more energy, lasts much longer, and becomes easier to produce, and that may take a long time. In the meantime, unsound legislation forces absurd economic practices such as in the Southwest where, at times, California literally pays Arizona to use its excess solar power. The intelligentsia and other elites should either get behind at least one viable alternative to solar in generating electricity or exclusively use unsubsidized solar power in their own lives, especially with their private jets.

41. CHESTERTON'S FENCE

IMAGINE A YOUNG MAN CROSSING some fields and coming to a fence. He looks and looks, and thinks and thinks, but simply cannot come up with a reason why the fence is there. After some consideration, he takes the fence down. The young man likely rationalized that someone saw an essential purpose for having a fence in that location; after all, they took the time to build it. But this young man could not fathom the purpose, and so he took it down. It is a story of arrogance, of someone thinking they know so much more than the people who came before them.

This little-known story comes from a book G.K. Chesterton wrote in 1929. The story has a broader meaning: the importance of respecting established institutions such as judicial systems, financial systems, property rights, and educational systems that have been developed through the ages. When the intelligentsia or anyone else abandons long-established institutions or encourages others to do the same, they are embarking on a course of action fraught with peril.

Of course, institutions need to change, and they do change through time. The question is: how does one effectively separate good changes from bad changes? Allowing each of the states in America to conduct their own experiments to modify important institutions is one answer. If a state makes an ineffective change, other states can learn from observing the experiments and the whole nation is not taken down by the mistake. But, if the federal government forces a change in an institution for all fifty states, it may not be clear whether the change was helpful because we cannot observe and compare the difference the change made between states anymore. Federal controls that force all states to behave identically eliminate the ability of the states to compete against each other to improve our lives.

Take another example: In the wake of the 2016 elections, many students complained that the Electoral College is a failure and should be abolished. Perhaps they are right. But these students did not see amending the Constitution as the pathway to their goal. They believed their preferences should rule and that the Constitution should step aside.

The arrogant intelligentsia and political elitists are trying to tear down our institutions and are making the same mistake the young man made in Chesterton's story. They should at least be required to pursue their changes via constitutional amendments rather than through activist judges.

42. Hating the Person in the Mirror

As a college professor for more than thirty years, I have seen a gradual transformation in the attitudes of my students toward wealth. Students increasingly see the wealthy as the leeches and those on government assistance as victims.

I often pose the following question: Suppose a corporation makes and sells a product with features that make the product less safe than it could be. Further, the corporation is aware of this when it decides to make the product and the sole reason for the decision was to enjoy better profit margins. Given these facts, and assuming the corporation's customers are unaware of these safety issues, would it be morally or legally wrong for the corporation to sell the product?

Virtually every student says the corporation is wrong and should be punished through litigation and constrained by regulation.

I then give my students a simple homework assignment. I ask them to construct a list of all the actions they take that are analogous to the actions of the corporation. In other words, what steps does an ordinary person take that (1) place other persons at added risk of injury or death, (2) do so without the knowledge of the persons being placed at risk, and (3) are done for the primary purpose of saving money?

The list of everything they come up with is long. For example, we don't think twice about driving an extra mile to buy products that are on sale, thereby increasing the chance we'll have a car accident. We go without expensive sprinkler systems in our houses and redundant brake systems in our cars. We drive fast to get to our job just so we can keep earning a salary. The list can go on and on because two things are clear; we prefer more money to less money, and making things as safe as possible costs a lot of money.

We are tolerant of other people behaving the same way we do because we identify with them. But people increasingly see corporations as their enemies and are quite willing to hold them to standards that both they and we are unwilling or unable to meet. Corporations are just legal abstractions. Ultimately, all decisions are made by people. All people should be held to the same standard, whether they are acting alone, as a worker, as an executive, or in any other role.

43. Is It Good to Have a King?

I FIND MODERN SOCIETY'S TENDENCY to fawn over royalty and despise the bourgeoisie perplexing. Take, for instance, the British monarchy. Billions of people follow their weddings and funerals as if these people were dear relatives who show them great kindnesses. In reality, royal families benefit from a despicable system. Royal families contribute nothing to economic growth while prospering entirely by their lineage. The great advances that have fed the world, cured diseases, and allowed the masses to live in comfort have been made despite, not because of, monarchies. In fact, monarchies prevented such advances for centuries. The common person through the ages was held hostage by royalty and forced into virtual servitude.

On the other hand, the bourgeoisie has led humanity out of those centuries of disease and poverty into the modern world of better nutrition, better health, and ever-increasing prosperity. Most people despise the great industrialists, past and present. Take Bill Gates, for example. People voluntarily buy Microsoft software because they think the benefits of owning the software exceed the cost of paying for it. Bill Gates and the employees of Microsoft spent incredible amounts of time and invested much talent and effort to develop products that make us happy. Occasionally, industrialists trick me, entrap me in their product lines, or prevent me from accessing the products of their competitors. But, generally speaking, they are an army of talented people working their butts off to develop some product we will see as so useful that we reward them by giving back to them a portion of the value we gain.

Imagine if an alien visited Earth and was told about two places: first, the motor vehicle department, an institution that helps customers complete their paperwork without regard to the financial interests of the department's owners; and second, an accounting firm that also assists customers in completing paperwork, but with the sole purpose of making money for the company's owners. Which place would the alien expect treats its customers better? The alien's guess would likely be that profit-driven firms abuse their customers. Typically, market forces drive businesses to treat people more nicely than government agencies that hold monopolistic power. Why then do people malign the profit motive so freely? Even Shakespeare looked down on the bourgeoisie through his portrayal of Shylock as a sadistic merchant out to con his fellow human beings. Could it be that consumers dislike merchants due to deep-seated jealousy that the merchant is making a profit? Wouldn't it then hold that citizens should dislike motor vehicle employees due to their job security and lavish benefits, such as health insurance and pension plans?

Stockholm syndrome is the tendency of some captives to have positive feelings toward their captors. Do free people have a similar, latent desire to be the subjects of kings and politicians, even though they'll be treated like customers at the motor vehicle department? Do they want to abdicate responsibility and avoid making decisions? Wouldn't it be better to be treated with respect by people working to serve us, even though they'll make a buck while doing so?

44. IS EVERYTHING RELATIVE?

I HAVE STUDIED RESEARCH THAT evaluates the relative ability of free market economies and socialist economies to generate economic growth. Free market economies generate more long-term prosperity for most citizens. But free markets also allow income inequality.

The intelligentsia and political elitists deem free markets immoral. In their view, something is moral if society deems it moral. I believe objective truth exists, although I do not claim to discern it perfectly.

Slavery is wrong, for example, but not just because contemporary society deems it wrong.

Most of my students are shocked to hear one of their professors use the words "right" and "wrong" in a moral discussion. By the time these students get to my class, professors have taught them for years that there is no such thing as right or wrong behavior; behavior either matches our beliefs or it does not.

I ask my students what they think would happen if they walked up to one of these professors and punched them in the mouth. Do they think the professor would say something like this: "Gee, thanks. Our opinions about violence differ, but I respect that and join you in celebrating our diversity in attitudes about the initiation of violence"? I believe the professor would call the campus police, insisting the student be punished because the student did something wrong.

Most liberal arts professors favor socialism and hate free markets. These intellectual elitists like to defend socialist policies on the grounds that they foster justice and promote equality. They bemoan wage inequality, although they reject the idea that the college's salary pool should be distributed equally among both faculty and staff because they somehow feel they should make more than staff. The intelligentsia wants to control the wealth.

From a pragmatic point of view, socialism has a slow but toxic effect on the long-term direction of an economy. In recent years, Venezuela has vividly demonstrated the long-term catastrophic results of rampant socialism. Although Venezuela is roughly tied with Saudi Arabia for possessing the world's largest proven oil reserves, since the socialists rose to full power in the late 1990s, Venezuela's oil exports have fallen by about 50 percent. While Venezuelan citizens struggle to obtain the necessities of life, the socialistic system has failed even to maintain the ability to extract oil from the ground.

I see a political pendulum at work throughout the world. When a country's economy languishes, the people tend to push their government toward free-market reforms to get the economy moving again. When a nation is economically thriving, its populace tends to call for socialistic leadership to reduce wealth inequality. Former UK Prime Minister Margaret Thatcher said, "The problem with socialism is that you eventually run out of other people's money."

But enough about pragmatism. Is an economic system that allows economic inequality moral? Absolutely. Our country was rightfully founded on equality under the law, not equality of outcomes. Socialism steals freedom from all and wealth from those who produce it. America was founded on principles of freedom and liberty. There is a process to amend our Constitution. Liberal judges, legislators, and executives are circumventing the Constitution and assuming socialistic powers. Will America's economic pendulum bring us back to the values that made the US the world leader in innovation? Some argue that America's interests should be "first." But America is on a long-term path to socialism and authoritarianism. Freedom should be first.

45. THE SOVIETS IN THE REARVIEW MIRROR

MY HIGH SCHOOL MATH AND science teachers seemed apolitical to me. But my English and social studies teachers were vocal about politics. In general, they were even-handed to a fault in their appraisal of communism vs. capitalism. They discussed the potential advantages and disadvantages of each economic system as if we were discussing the pros and cons of paper bags vs. plastic bags. I entered college believing the right economic path lay between communism and capitalism.

These teachers' views merely reflected those of the world's intellectual elites. The most renowned economist of that era was

94

Paul Samuelson of MIT. Samuelson authored the seminal textbook, *Economics: An Introductory Analysis*. That textbook became the font of received economic wisdom for tens of millions of Americans.

Throughout the 1960s and 1970s, each new edition of Samuelson's text continued to forecast that the Soviet economy would grow to the size of the US economy within the next two to three decades. The US economy was roughly twice the size of the Soviet economy in 1960, but, even though it remained so through 1980, Samuelson continued to predict the Soviets would catch up. How could America's first recipient of the Nobel Prize in Economics be so wrong for so many years? The world's greatest economists, then as now, have not fully appreciated the role of market prices in communicating accurate information about the value of resources. The Soviets tried to navigate a technologically changing economy without using market prices. By not allowing free markets, they denied themselves the information that market prices could have disseminated, and their economy stagnated.

Even in the 1960s, an economy was too complicated to be run efficiently by central planning. More than fifty years later technology, and thus the economy, has exploded in complexity. For example, back in the 1960s I had access to only two television channels. Most television programs ran virtually unchanged for many years in their casts and formats. Television programming would not have been so complicated for a central planner to oversee in 1960. But now, most people in the developed world have access to hundreds of channels. Further, changes in programming on each channel are rapid. Imagine how unmanageable even just this sliver of a large modern economy would be to a single group of people trying to decide what programming people want and how to give it to them most efficiently.

Central planning fails both when applied to an entire economy and to just specific economic sectors. With luck, the elite economists of tomorrow and the teachers who learn from them will see the ever-growing complexity of the economy and bury the argument that central planning is an efficient model for running a modern economy, just like capitalism has buried socialism.

46. Prices as an Information Freeway

THE WAY MARKET PRICES GUIDE an economy is beautiful. No elite government body can possibly understand how to evaluate benefits and costs as effectively and quickly as a multitude of common people who make independent decisions based on free-market prices.

Few people know this but, for years, many dental offices have saved the waste from their sinks and floors and sold it to entrepreneurs who collect the waste for its silver and gold content. The entrepreneurs don't need to know anything about precious metals or dentistry; all they need to know is the cost to obtain the waste, the cost of getting the waste to the smelters, and the price paid to them by the smelters. The smelter only needs to know the cost of smelting and the market prices of the precious metals they recover.

Each person in this or any other economic process needs to know two things: market prices and their own ability to perform the required tasks. People are experts in their fields. For example, the people in the dentist's office know how much cost is involved in collecting the waste. The people in the smelting plant know what is involved in processing the material. But these people do not know what the other people are doing or what their costs are. So how does the system work? In a free market, the entire process is guided by information contained in market prices. No government bureaucrat could possibly collect and understand the information necessary to make these decisions wisely.

And, everything changes through time. Silver and gold are giving way to composite dental materials. People are recognizing the toxicity of mercury and our need to exert care in its disposal. The industry that collects and processes dental waste is changing in response. And the information that says "change is needed" is communicated quickly and automatically through changes in the market prices of precious metals, as well as everything else involved, such as the gasoline used in transporting the materials and the natural gas used in smelting the materials. All those prices guide the parties involved to make socially beneficial decisions, so the pie gets bigger.

The network of people and organizations that collect and process dental waste is nimble, quickly making changes when the changes can make our economy more efficient. This is all done continuously through the power of self-interest and the information provided by market prices. Can we be confident these market prices are being expertly determined? Yes. Thousands of industry experts and financial traders are scrutinizing market prices, such as precious metal prices, minute by minute, looking for market prices that are incorrectly balancing supply and demand. There is no mastermind orchestrating everyone and everything. This ability of a free society to self-organize into a super-efficient economy is a thing of great beauty.

The failure of centrally planned economies throughout history shows that government bureaucrats cannot organize an economy through coercion as effectively as people can on a voluntary basis. Even if bureaucrats were somehow able to perform a thorough analysis and determine an appropriate set of prices, their work would soon become obsolete as technology changes. Countries with moderate socialism survive in the modern world only because they can observe the market prices generated by free exchange. If all free market economies become socialized, the world will lose its information system and our economic progress will reverse into economic decay.

47. LESSONS LEARNED IN SUNDAY SCHOOL BY THE TEACHER

YEARS AGO, I SERVED AS a fifth-grade teacher in Sunday school and learned this important principle: we should allow people the freedom to create value and ensure that people who create value can retain their wealth.

I learned this from a major project. The class needed to make a lot of cards for people in a nursing home, and we found an easy solution: reward the kids for making the cards. We used candy. But there was another important element: we didn't allow kids to steal the cards from other kids who made them. You had to make it yourself to get the candy. Since the children felt they would receive the fruits of their labor, there was peace. Some children innovated and developed ways of making the cards; other children quickly adopted the innovations. I was surprised by how well they cooperated. Each child made as many cards as he or she wished and had no reason to interfere with their peers.

But, if we had allowed theft, all sorts of things would have gone wrong. The victims would have wasted time trying to protect their cards from theft. The thieves would have wasted time trying to find ways to steal the cards. All the kids would have begun to lobby me and the other authorities to receive protection or favor. Or, worst of all, the honest kids would have stopped making cards out of fear that other kids would steal them.

In life as an adult, corrupt governments allow their cronies to steal from productive people. In socialist governments, the government itself does the stealing. In either case, the incentives to produce are diminished. People turn their natural desire to improve their lives to the political process rather than the productive process. And the pie gets smaller.

America is weathering a storm of "smash and grab." We have always faced thieves who literally smash windows and steal. But, increasingly, the smashing and grabbing are being done openly by high-level politicians and community organizers. The tactic is simple: first, harness the power of government to smash—or threaten to smash—a successful business, then agree to "call off the dogs" if the business bribes the politicians, makes campaign donations, or makes donations to key community organizations. The strategy can even be applied to a scheme to drive down the market price of the business's stock so that it can be accumulated cheaply.

48. THE HUTTERITES AND THE SHAKERS

THE HUTTERITES AND THE SHAKERS can each teach us valuable lessons. Both are American religious groups, and both tend to live in small communities and interact primarily with other group members. Their histories provide insight into economic systems.

Shakers are famous for making furniture with simple designs. They live communally and practice pacifism and celibacy. What was that last thing? Celibacy. You might ask how a community that practices celibacy is sustainable. It isn't, although for a while they adopted orphans. There's only one Shaker community left, and it's all but gone. I think their pacifism and communal living were equally unsustainable but, even if they fixed those problems, celibacy would still have been their demise.

Like the Shakers, the Hutterites are pacifists who generally practice communal living. But, owing to their lack of celibacy, they are not perishing. The Hutterites have one really good idea: when one of their groups (colonies) becomes too big, it must break itself into two groups by creating a daughter colony.

Whether by luck or by wisdom, the Hutterites have adopted a very sensible plan. As populations grow, voluntary communal living will fail because the members no longer feel a tight bond with each other and no longer know each other personally. The usual way to retain the members of very large communal groups is by force: people cannot exit. The Hutterites divide, thereby conquering many problems.

I am shocked by the indifference Americans show to the plight of Cubans, Venezuelans, and North Koreans who are not free to flee from their countries. Communal living on a large scale is a disaster. To maintain it requires the government to control its population with terror—especially through violence—to prevent them from leaving the country. How could any freedom-loving American admire what Fidel Castro and similar dictators have done to their people? It is appalling to me. But the intelligentsia are silent about these atrocities.

Free countries allow their citizens to experiment with different lifestyles and be free to leave the community, just like free economies allow entrepreneurs to experiment with new technologies and be free to exit a market. The key in both cases is to allow freedom and avoid micromanagement. In the long run, good ideas will thrive and bad ideas will perish, as long as the bad ideas are not kept going through subsidies raised by taking money from those with good ideas.

But most politicians prefer to tax good ideas and subsidize bad ideas. That was a recipe for disaster in the 1960s—when huge American corporate conglomerates propped up their worst-performing divisions by raiding the coffers of their best-performing divisions. The result was that corporate America lost most of its competitiveness. And it will be a disaster for this country if politicians are allowed to micromanage our society through taxation and spending practices that penalize the functional and subsidize the dysfunctional.

It is foolish to apply the micromanagement approach of small communes to large, modern economies. Economies thrive with a hands-off approach that allows individuals to make their own economic decisions and pursue goals they set for themselves. It means trusting that farmers will produce enough of each type of food to feed the entire society without government quotas. It means that automobile manufacturers, house builders, and producers in every other industry who are able to survive competitive pressures will tend to excel at meeting consumer needs without government subsidies. It means some people with poor educations will be in charge of large businesses rather than the intelligentsia. But it works through the miracle of markets, the creativity of some entrepreneurs, and the wisdom of consumers to know what they want.

49. OUR YOUTH SHOULD PROTECT THEIR FUTURE

IF CANDLE MAKERS AND WHALERS had had their way in the 19th century, we would still be living without electric lights. We need to be vigilant that politicians don't crush the innovations of today and the future.

My son has traveled the world at low cost using services such as Uber and Airbnb. In addition to seeing his expenses slashed, he's enjoyed meeting the providers of these services. The online services allow for screening based on the reputations they've gained through online reviews. These internet-based enterprises allow people with excess room in their cars or homes to provide rides and housing to people wishing to avoid the high costs of taxis and hotels. Other entrepreneurs serve gourmet meals in their homes or yours with substantial economic benefits. Imagine a day in America when we will get more use from our cars and when there are fewer cars on the road because more and more cars will be carrying more than one person. The eventual implications of these sharing services are unimaginable now.

Most powerful innovations disrupt the world. They create many losers in the short run. People tend to lose their jobs and businesses when someone else finds a better way to meet consumer needs. We can only implement improved ways of doing things if we stop doing them the old way. This means some people suffer when their services become obsolete. But innovations don't violate anyone's natural rights. The business owners and workers who can't stay competitive are not victims. Just because their ways of providing value have become inefficient, they have no natural right to halt progress and prevent new businesses and workers from taking their turn. The America of the future will thrive or falter based on whether we allow innovation.

In a way, the battles erupting between new firms like Uber and old firms such as taxi companies comprise a war pitting the people losing from innovation against those benefiting from it. The youth will be waging a battle against the establishment for huge stakes—their ability to shape their own world.

The new firms' apps fit neatly into the preferences of millennials. Unlike their parents, millennials have little or no interest in accumulating suburban homes, vacation houses, and multiple cars. Millennials have deferred having children. They prefer to rent small apartments in urban areas and travel at low cost.

More generally, we can hardly imagine the future of the game-changing innovations a world of billions of people can create, especially with 3D printing. I remember in the late 1960s going to the public library to use what, by today's standards, was a slow, expensive, low-grade photocopying machine. But, back then, it was a time-saving breakthrough. I could never have imagined I would someday own an inexpensive, high-quality copier for my own home. Will 3D printing follow a similar path? Will nanotechnology merge with 3D printing to create a world of low-cost, high-quality, home-based manufacturing? No one knows, yet the intelligentsia and crony capitalists want to control the innovations.

The youth should realize the stakes: if the establishment wins, they will lose their ability to create the world of their dreams. And they will lose opportunities that none of us can yet imagine. Our youth must fight for their rights to innovate on their pathways to accomplish their dreams, and then protect the rights of their children to do the same.

50. WHY NOT A $50 PER HOUR MINIMUM WAGE?

AN INCREASING PROPORTION OF STUDENTS entering my classes hold these two beliefs: first, increasing the minimum wage helps the poor, unskilled, and young; and second, people who disagree with a proposal to raise the minimum wage don't care about the poor, the unskilled, and the young.

It's easy to shake their confidence that increasing the minimum wage would help the poor, the unskilled, and the young. In my class, I propose we raise the minimum hourly wage to $50, and I invite a discussion about what would happen. They come to recognize the results: many jobs would disappear, and the few remaining jobs would go only to the most skilled and qualified applicants—or those with family connections. With few employers able to pay $50 an hour, the least skilled workers wouldn't be able to compete. Without the minimum wage, unskilled workers can compete for jobs by accepting lower wages. So the minimum wage of $50 per hour would hurt a lot of people, especially the very people the legislators intend to help.

The debate isn't about whether we care about the poor. Some people care more about the poor than others, and they show it by making personal sacrifices for their beliefs. But supporting a high minimum wage doesn't demonstrate love for the poor. Most people think that higher minimum wages come out of the pockets of the rich business owners. In a free market, the higher wages are paid by customers through higher prices.

The intelligentsia denigrate employers who pay low wages to their employees, even though elites prefer to engage in academic and policy work rather than invest their own time and money in starting businesses that pay high wages to unskilled workers. If they don't have the desire or skill to start such a business then we should at least expect that they will pay hefty wages to the people for childcare, lawn work, and house cleaning. They don't. Ask a laborer about the types of people who treat them poorly. The intelligentsia are not saints.

Every economist teaches that raising the price of something normally causes demand to decline. They promote high taxes on cigarettes and other "sins" in part because it will discourage consumption. But liberal economists seem to throw this economic principle away when discussing the minimum wage. They claim that raising the price of unskilled labor (i.e., raising the minimum wage) will have little or no effect on how much unskilled labor the employers will demand. That is nonsense. Unbiased, comprehensive, and sound evidence from Seattle's experiences and elsewhere demonstrate the opposite: unskilled laborers lose out. But that is how the elitists operate—they ignore any logic or evidence that does not fit into their agenda.

High minimum wages don't solve the problems of unskilled, economically disadvantaged young people. But they do have four effects:

1. They drive up the prices of the goods and services unskilled workers help produce, thereby reducing the demand for those goods and services and, in turn, reducing the demand for unskilled workers;

2. Those higher prices for goods and services impact poor people, such as unskilled workers, more than most others, because they are least able to afford higher prices and tend to shop at businesses that hire minimum wage workers;

3. They encourage employers to innovate to reduce the size of their workforce. (That may increase overall economic efficiency, but the increased efficiency comes at the expense of the least skilled people who get left out of work.); and

4. They encourage employers to offer their skilled employees more hours (because of wage compression and the relatively higher productivity of skilled workers), resulting in less hours for the workers who don't make the cut.

A compassionate way to help those who struggle to get by would, counterintuitively, be to eliminate the minimum wage and thereby legalize low-wage workers. Unskilled workers should be allowed their right to compete by accepting lower wages to get their start in the workforce.

51. THE BOTTOM LINE

THE PATHWAY TO PROSPERITY FOR an economy can be summarized in a simple flowchart. Let's start at the top with the purpose of an economy: meeting our needs and wants. Most people want health, longevity, education, medical care, dental care, good nutrition, entertainment, and so forth. What enables people to meet these needs and wants? Wealth is key. Most people in wealthy societies have better access to meeting these needs and wants than most people in impoverished societies. The flowchart depicts the foundation to achieving our economic goals.

Wealth comes from productivity—the process of creating value. High levels of productivity come from economic efficiency—the process of making the most of our labor and other resources. Efficiency comes from technology. Advancements in technology have enabled the US to reduce its agricultural workforce from well over 50 percent of its labor pool to under 3 percent in just the last 125 years. Mankind experienced thousands of years of struggling just to feed its population—and then, within a single century, the US increased its food production to the point that it can feed everyone using less than one-tenth of its previous workforce. How does this progress happen? Here's the full flowchart starting at the top with our ultimate goals:

Our Needs and Wants
↑
Wealth
↑
Productivity
↑
Efficiency
↑
Technology
↑
Specialization
↑
Trade
↑
Natural Rights
(Especially private property rights)

What causes technology to advance? As depicted above, technology comes from people being able to specialize in the quest to develop better methods of doing more and doing better. But specialization can only take place when people are able to trade. Trade allows people to meet their need for income and diverse consumption while concentrating on a specialty. But it is through specialization and trade that entrepreneurs and other creators of technology can tap into the expertise of other specialists.

Finally, it is obvious that there can be nothing to trade unless people are free to own property and to transfer those private property rights to others. More important, there is no incentive to trade, specialize, innovate, or improve unless, in doing so, one retains the right to reap the rewards.

What is government's role in all this? All the government needs to do is this: protect—rather than infringe upon—the natural rights of its citizens. Governments infringe on natural rights when they subsidize the technologies prized by government bureaucrats, when they protect their cronies, and when they preserve outdated methods.

People often claim that figuring out how much government is optimal is a very difficult task. But it is easy to agree on a reasonable size for government when government's role is focused on protecting the natural rights of its citizens rather than infringing upon them. Simply put, we need powerful government to protect our natural rights and limited government that does anything else.

52. In the Cosmic Scheme of Things

In September 1962, President Kennedy called for the United States to put a man on the moon (and return him safely) by the end of the decade. This was an incredibly ambitious goal at that time because the

US space program was quite primitive. Serious hurdles remained. But America did it.

In January 2004, President George W. Bush proposed returning to the moon with manned spacecraft by the year 2020, 16 years from his speech. Now let's check the facts. America reached the moon less than seven years after Kennedy's speech, and additional trips to the moon were successfully completed in the 1970s. More than 34 years later, Bush proposed doing it again, but figured that this time it would take 16 years to do it! Bush's goal turned out to be a "mis-underestimation."

Think of all the gains in technology, especially rocket engines and computers, that transpired in the intervening 34 years between late 1969 and early 2004. Think of all the money NASA spent in those years on rocket technology, yet the task of getting to the moon had become more onerous! This example highlights how technological progress can be reversed—not just halted—when the institutions supporting an economy deteriorate.

But there is hope. In February 2018, Elon Musk's SpaceX demonstrated the ability to bring two unmanned rocket boosters back to a precise and simultaneous upright landing after sending a rocket into space. Musk's SpaceX program is leapfrogging NASA in technology despite NASA's bloated budget—which seems increasingly devoted to funding global climate change discussions.

Musk is not alone. Other privately funded entrepreneurs are racing to explore space in a competitive frenzy reminiscent of the race to improve aircraft in the decades after the Wright brothers' inaugural flight in 1903. It has been entrepreneurs, not government bureaucrats, that have driven the last two centuries of technological progress. More amazingly, technological progress is rapidly accelerating. It merely requires a society that respects each other's natural rights to life, liberty and the pursuit of happiness.

Economic change and technological advancements occurred very slowly for millennia up until the late 18th century. It has only been in the last 200 years that man has traveled hundreds of miles per hour, flown, reached the moon, transplanted organs, communicated electronically, and created artificial lighting. Societies in previous millennia struggled just trying to produce enough food to stave off major waves of starvation.

According to historians, the most notable people from the centuries prior to 1800 were government leaders, religious leaders, philosophers, scientists, and writers. But, in the last two centuries, the most influential and notable people are dominated by inventors and entrepreneurs. I think one of the most notable people of all time is alive today: the first person to walk on another planet (presumably Mars). This is especially true if that person will also have played a key role in making the first manned mission to Mars possible. Elon Musk may pass all others as the most notable figure in all human history.

53. Strong Fences Make Good Neighbors

AMERICA IS DEEPLY DIVIDED. THE problem is not that we have many major differences. The seriousness of the divide emanates from one underlying problem, which is that many Americans no longer respect the natural rights of others. Natural rights serve as fences that limit the extent to which government can be used to mold people into accommodating the preferences of others. When we abandon the preeminence of natural rights, we are no longer safe from those who want to enslave others to their will. These fences protect people, allowing them to prosper, create, cooperate, and support each other. The fences diminish our conflicts with, and our hatred for, one another.

We can see the importance of natural rights in nature. Strong predatory animals such as bears, eagles, and wolverines respect each other's natural rights. They have territories within their domains in which they are safe and which they defend, if necessary, from others. Within that territory, they build their dens or nests and raise their offspring. They cooperate socially outside these borders on some occasions, such as when mating or congregating in locations with a dense availability of food, but they generally respect each other's boundaries and are safe from each other up to the point of a border dispute. They may fight, but most of the time they live in peace.

The importance of natural rights even among animals is not limited to predators. Prey animals have also developed systems to enable their survival. Herds of mammals, flocks of birds, and schools of fish have evolved with systems of social "fences" within which they can peacefully cooperate. These animals have developed innate systems of natural rights because they are the fittest systems of survival.

America has thrived for more than two-and-a-half centuries based on protections set in place when our government was founded. The preeminence of natural rights in this book mirrors the emphasis on natural rights that permeated the work of America's founding fathers.

The key is to respect the natural rights of others and, in so doing, limit the extent to which we are allowed to impose our beliefs on others. Americans were right two centuries ago when they began the process of protecting the natural rights of people to be free from enslavement. Americans were right decades ago when they insisted on the protection of the natural rights of each citizen in the privacy of their homes and bedrooms to exercise their consensual sexual practices free of government persecution. The reason is that sex is a natural right among consenting adults.

But Americans are wrong when they invade the workplace to micromanage hiring practices, firing practices, and the specifics of compensation arrangements. Americans are wrong when they deny access to medicine and medical devices of choice to other Americans. Americans are wrong to impose ever-changing gender beliefs on other Americans, such as prescribing how many bathrooms must be built on someone else's property. Americans are wrong to punish or assault other Americans who exercise their natural right to free speech when that speech poses no clear and present danger to the natural rights of others.

The list goes on and on, and it all leads to the place where we find ourselves today: many people are using the force of government to impose their political beliefs on others, irrespective of natural rights. They are tearing down the strong fences that make us good neighbors and, in doing so, are destroying this great nation.

54. TOO BIG TO FAIL

ALMOST HALF OF AMERICANS PAY no federal income tax. Many have negative federal income tax payments because they receive earned-income tax credits—cash from the government. Much of the federal income tax collected each year is paid by less than ten percent of the population. But, instead of expressing gratitude to the rich for the disproportionate share they pay, lots of people complain that the rich still don't pay enough in taxes. When you quiz these complainers about how much each income group pays in income taxes, they do not even know; they simply believe they should have the right to pay less.

But the real problem is not the distribution of the tax burden; it is the growing size of the tax burden. Government's share of the economic pie keeps growing at the federal, state, and local levels. Consider the multitude of taxes we now face: income taxes (federal, state, and sometimes local), property taxes, estate taxes, licensing fees, sales taxes, tolls, real estate transfer taxes, unemployment taxes, Social Security taxes, Medicare taxes, environmental disposal fees, rental car taxes, lodging taxes, and utility taxes.

Taxation is increasingly a power struggle that pits elements of our society against each other. The animosity of this political debate grows. The divisions between Americans keep growing deeper and deeper due to the increasing belief that the economic pie is fixed and that, if one group can claim a bigger piece of the pie, then someone else has to have a smaller piece. But, if we unleash economic growth rather than taxing it to death, then the pie will get bigger and the income of all classes can grow. And that is exactly what has happened through time. Poor Americans enjoy lifestyles that the richest people in the world did not possess 150 years ago: fresh food year-round, electric lighting, air conditioning, motorized transportation, vastly improved medical and dental care, and electronic access to incredible quantities of information and entertainment.

We need to return to viewing taxation as a necessary evil that should be used sparingly, applied in ways that encourage value creation, and levied to create benefits for everyone, not employed as a tool for some people to make themselves better off at the expense of others. The former nurtures unity; the latter creates class warfare.

People complain, rightfully so, about the corruption and dysfunction within our governments. The bigger problem with our governments is that they have become too powerful. States with low salaries for legislators, such as New Hampshire, Tennessee, and Texas tend to have little or no income tax. Conversely, highly taxed states such as California pay their legislators the highest salaries. We need to reduce the incentives that make government bigger. Otherwise, we will end up like the impending disaster known as California.

55. Giving Credit Where Credit Is Due

SOME PEOPLE BELIEVE GOVERNMENT (IN general) and politicians (in particular) feed the hungry and house the homeless. But it is farmers who produce food and construction workers who build shelters. More important, it is taxpayers who pay the farmers and construction workers to serve the needs of the poor. All the politicians do is vote for the taxes or the loans to finance these projects. Instead of naming buildings and highways for politicians who vote for higher taxes, increased borrowing, and more spending, I would like to see the structures named for the biggest taxpayers.

People who raise money for charities are only part of the success stories. The people who make the donations deserve much of the credit. In fact, I'd like to see the participants in walk-a-thons do something value-creating to get sponsored, like picking up litter or planting trees.

Social media is buzzing with young voters and others who proudly proclaim their allegiance to politicians who support expanded social programs. But most of these young voters are low-income earners who pay virtually no income tax. It is the high-income workers who foot the bill for the largess of the liberals. Yet high-income taxpayers are disdained rather than honored. The underlying belief of these young voters is that high-income taxpayers are not generating value, that they are somehow grabbing pieces of a pie they did not create. Based on my years of experience with these young voters, I can say with confidence that they do not know what they are talking about.

Liberals have it backward. They claim that the poor are the victims of a free market. Nothing could be further from the truth. The victims of our society are not those who live on the public dole. The real victims are those who create enormous value by being innovative

113

and efficient producers, only to see their hard-earned money handed out to able-bodied loafers.

Progressive leftists have indoctrinated our youth through the education system to believe that every poor person is a victim. They view homelessness in America as resulting from a recent crisis, such as being fired from a job. I often ask my students this: imagine that you lost your job, your life savings, your car, your house or apartment, and all of your other possessions. Would you be forced into homelessness? Think about it. How many people do you know who would be willing to let you live with them until you got back on your feet financially? The answer is dozens: relatives, friends, past roommates, neighbors, former co-workers, former teachers, etc. And there are charities willing to help the poor. The point is this: these people on the street either chose to be there, or they have "burned every bridge" in their past relationships.

I frequent a New England college town that has young adults begging on the main streets and at almost every intersection. The same beggars are there day after day. The rich are not like you and me, and neither are these beggars. Our charity toward them should be based on a sober view of whether or not our attempts to extend mercy are encouraging them to waste their lives.

56. TRUSTING A BEAR TO BE A BEAR

MANY OF US ATTEMPT TO control others because we do not trust their intentions. Let's think about whether we trust bears. In one sense, we cannot trust a bear. Bears have been known to attack people. But, in another sense, we can trust a bear. We can trust a bear to be a bear. We trust that the bear cannot fly, does not carry a gun, and rarely seeks confrontation with a human.

When it comes to people, can we trust that a person will be altruistic? No. People are altruistic some of the time, but I do not trust people to be altruistic very often. For example, I do not trust that truck drivers will transport food to my local stores every day, year after year, out of altruism. I believe their primary motivation is self-interest. They want to earn a living.

Every day I count on farmers, manufacturers, transportation workers, store clerks, and others to bring food and other items that I need for survival. Am I trusting in their altruism or their self-interest? I am reminded of the sign some store owners post: *In God We Trust: All Others Pay Cash.* Self-interest is a good and natural force. We trust the self-interest of others to motivate them to go to work each day and keep our economy running. Our survival depends on their self-interest as well as our own.

Our society goes through periods in which self-interest is maligned. The late 1960s and 1970s formed an era in which altruism was widely praised over self-interest. Yet that era also saw high levels of domestic terrorism in the United States from radical groups supporting anarchy, civil rights, an end to war, Puerto Rican independence, etc. These terrorists and violent protestors were altruistic, risking their lives and freedom to pursue what they perceived as greater goals. Even when altruism prevails, it may be in the form of a malicious force.

The key to self-interest in a free market economy is that it guides producers into serving other people's preferences and serving them as efficiently as possible. The most self-interested business owners provide the goods and services customers most want to buy, not what they think people ought to buy. I, for one, want producers to meet my preferences. I like a business that bends over backward to make me happy, even if it makes a buck in the process. In centrally managed economies, producers have a powerful incentive to make their products undesirable so they will not be burdened by excess demand and criticized for their inability to meet demand. In centrally managed economies, participants seek to curry favor with government authorities rather than their fellow citizens.

We trust bees to be bees. That means we take precautions against being stung and we try to prevent them from living too close to where our children play. But bees are essential to pollination, and we trust bees to pollinate many of our sources of food. Bees do not pollinate because they love people and want people to have enough food to eat. Bees pollinate because it is an unintended consequence of their real objective: obtaining food. Similarly, free market producers do a great job of providing for our society. There is nothing wrong—and much right—about them doing it for their own happiness. Our price system communicates our preferences, and the self-interest of those producers motivates them to meet those preferences efficiently.

The intelligentsia and political elite malign the self-interest of others ad nauseam, not realizing that, to the extent they succeed in restricting self-interest, they will be biting the hand that feeds them.

57. THE FDA AS AMERICA'S KILLING MACHINE

I OFTEN ASK MY STUDENTS about the implications of typical statements made by the FDA (the Food and Drug Administration). For example, what do they think it means when the FDA announces that, after ten years of rigorous study, it has approved a drug that will prevent more than 10,000 premature deaths per year? After discussion, students eventually realize that the FDA's statement is an admission, that over the last ten years, it has killed more than 100,000 Americans by denying them legal access to the new medicine.

Still, too many Americans support the FDA's authority to prevent the ill from getting medicines or medical devices it hasn't yet approved. They claim the moral right to prevent the ill from seeking innovative treatments to their own bodies. Those who have empowered the FDA with its current authority and those who lead the FDA are responsible for the sickness and death of millions of people each year who could potentially be helped by interventions not yet approved.

There have been exciting developments in the treatment of diabetes, for example, including approaches that integrate continuous glucose monitoring with automatic insulin-delivery systems. But, in a nation that prides itself on being the land of the free, it has been illegal for medical firms to distribute lifesaving diabetes products until the FDA has completed its interminable testing. In the meantime, diabetics are suffering from erratic insulin levels because of bureaucrats' vain hope that the devices can be improved to the point of being near perfect and idiot-proof.

Americans sometimes can't even escape the FDA by going abroad. While some patients travel to other countries for treatment, many large companies fear the FDA, quite wisely, and determine there's too much to risk selling their devices or medicines to Americans abroad.

How did we end up with such a powerful authority? It began with the Pure Food and Drug Act of 1906. The FDA's original purpose was to prevent the interstate sale of mislabeled drugs and foods. It's a reasonable interpretation of the Interstate Commerce Clause to allow the FDA to prevent interstate commercial fraud because prevention of fraud encourages commerce. But government has a natural tendency to seek greater power, so now the FDA has well over 10,000 employees and a budget of over $5 billion. No one can pretend the FDA is merely fighting fraud. There is nothing in the Constitution to support this power grab.

It may be reasonable to require warning labels and similar procedures that protect the imprudent from buying useless or dangerous drugs or devices. Better yet, the FDA or private entities could perform research and simply publish their findings rather than using force to prevent their usage. Perhaps a compromise would require companies to publish warnings from the FDA on their labels, as adults should have the right to make their own decisions about which medicines and medical procedures to use. We should all be concerned when any government agency takes away so much of our freedom to make our own choices about our health.

58. Odds Are That Prices Tell Us a Lot

Suppose you were in charge of a sports tournament and needed to place participating teams in brackets based on their strength. In other words, you need to rank the teams from most likely to win to least likely to win. How would you make the decisions? What information would you use to make the decision? Would you ask a number of sports writers? How about the coaches? Would computerized rankings be best?

If it were me, I would use the prices implicit in the betting odds in Las Vegas. The odds represent what the world's best sports analysts conclude when their financial future is on the line. To some, Las Vegas sports gambling conjures up images of gruff bookies focused on making sure bets balance out so that, no matter which team wins, the casino is guaranteed its take. But one of my colleagues who has been behind the scenes in Vegas sports betting, discovered that it's an increasingly sophisticated business—with the managers who oversee the betting operations continuously monitoring and collecting odds and point spreads from throughout the world using the internet and analyzing the data with sophisticated computer programs. These managers want access to the best information and they want it processed with speed and precision. They act more and more like wizards of the financial world.

Polls of coaches and sports writers would not be my primary source of information. Sportswriters and coaches are not financially account-able for making poor predictions on which teams are strongest. They can vote for their favorite teams with no consequence. But the people who run sports betting pay the price for their mistakes.

Some of my students bet on sports, and they recognize the accu-racy of the point spreads and odds offered in Las Vegas. They've learned the hard way that the odds and point spreads used in gam-bling on sports reflect reliable indications of the relative skill of the teams involved. It's become evident to them that, to consistently win at sports betting, they would have to have access to vital information that is not well known.

The same holds for prices in financial markets. People who believe that, with a little upfront study and a little ongoing research, they can identify underpriced stocks and increase their investment returns are usually fooling themselves. It is true that investors are wise to search for mutual funds with lower expense ratios, but that is not because markets do not reflect fair values. It is because different investment companies charge different levels of fees.

Many of my students hate when I talk about the difficulty of earning superior investment returns by trying to select underpriced stocks and bonds. They do not want to believe that the market prices of stocks and bonds adjust quickly to reflect changes in the underlying value of each investment. They fight tenaciously against the concept of financial market efficiency—the idea that you get what you pay for in investing directly in financial markets. They want to believe that they can consistently earn exceptional returns.

Financial markets do not offer ordinary investors the chance to consistently beat the market because the world's most talented investment professionals are already competing intensely to find superior rates of return. I know from experience. I've competed as an investor and as a money manager. I've also competed in other ways throughout my life, including as an intercollegiate swimmer and a tournament chess player. The skill and competition in financial markets surpass that in any other arena I have experienced. It's because the stakes are so huge. Financial markets attract the world's top talents and provide them with resources and incentives to devote all their energy to their work.

This financial competition benefits all of us. It means the prices that guide our nation's economic decisions, just like the point spreads and odds in sports betting, are as accurate as humanly possible.

59. MORAVIANS IN EARLY AMERICA

I LIVED FOR TWO DECADES in Bethlehem, Pennsylvania. Bethlehem was established in 1741 by a small group of Moravians. They were Protestants who fled Europe seeking religious liberty. They established several communities in the area (including Emmaus and Nazareth) and adopted a largely communal lifestyle for several decades. Residents lived in large buildings segregated by gender and marital status. Children were raised collectively by young, single women. Residents weren't allowed contact with outsiders. If a resident wished to buy goods from outsiders or sell goods to outsiders, they had to do so through the "outsider store."

After about twenty years, Bethlehem grew in population to several thousand, and the closed and communal lifestyle was largely abandoned. Today, the role of the Moravian churches in the community is quite similar to the role of other churches, such as the Methodists and Presbyterians.

Early Moravian settlers had a unity of purpose. They also had a faith-inspired work ethic, sense of discipline, sense of community, and devotion to living in a spirit of cooperation and love. But voluntary communal living is tenuous at best. Voluntary communes fall victim to disputes, deaths of charismatic founders, economic strife and, in some cases, becoming too large to support a feeling of closeness among the entire group.

My hometown is about forty miles from Ithaca, New York, home to Cornell University. The area surrounding Ithaca has been the site of numerous experiments in communal living. A small bunch of optimistic and enthusiastic young people would gather around an inspirational leader and pool their funds to establish a commune on a small farm. These communes usually got off to a good start based on positive attitudes, hard work, and lots of love and respect for each other. But most such experiments ended in financial ruin and interpersonal conflict.

Some small, family-oriented, communal arrangements work. But large-scale communal living generally fails because commune members lack familial connections. The failed economies of many highly socialistic nations are evidence that communal arrangements are not effective in large, diverse populations over long periods.

Years ago, when the Iron Curtain came down, my classes began attracting immigrants from formerly communist countries. I was surprised they tended to believe the Berlin Wall was erected to keep Westerners out rather than Easterners in. Apparently, they didn't know the guards had their guns pointing into their country. Almost no one was trying to flee the West.

I learned how difficult and fearful their lives had been. Their experiences were similar, despite their coming from different communist countries. I remember privately asking one Chinese student who was particularly reluctant to speak in class, "When you were in school in China, did you feel free to disagree with things your teacher was saying?" The student was confused by the question. He thought I was asking him whether he'd dare speak to another student or a family member about such a matter. He could not fathom the idea of directly confronting his teacher. Students who questioned authority could be forced to attend extra indoctrination programs. But worse for these students was the fear that an act of rebellion could be met with government reprisals against their parents, such as by setting them back in their careers.

The interpersonal conflict at Ithaca and Bethlehem's voluntary communes paled in comparison to what happens when communal arrangements are compulsory, which is necessary when communalism is implemented for the long term and on a large scale.

60. Is the Quality of US Health Care Falling?

Students are being indoctrinated with a pessimistic and hateful view of Western culture that includes the untenable declaration that the quality of health care in the United States is in steep decline. I have asked students about this. They are not just claiming that health care is becoming less affordable or more difficult to access; they are claiming that Americans are suffering longer recovery periods and less favorable outcomes each year for all the major maladies, such as cancer, heart disease, and stroke. They are learning this from listening to the intelligentsia and elitists that dominate university faculties.

They could not be more misinformed. One simple proof is this: go to Google, search for cancer survival rates, and click on images to see the graphs. Survival rates for the major categories of cancer are rising steadily (except in rare cases such as pancreatic cancer where the progress is slow). And this miraculous progress is not limited to cancer treatments. Stroke death rates are falling, heart disease treatments are improving, and on and on the improvements go. The rich travel to the United States from all over the world to get cutting-edge treatments for serious illnesses.

On what basis can a student examine the evidence and reach the conclusion that the quality of treatments is broadly declining? The answer is that they only read or hear about the few statistics that appear to support their beliefs. For example, whenever medical advances reduce the rates of death from one cause, by definition there must be an offsetting increase in death rates from other causes because the total death rate remains stubbornly fixed at 100 percent. So, the "doom and gloom" crowd can always find a medical statistic that appears to support their negativity. For example, if deaths from heart disease are delayed for several decades through miraculous treatments, statistics can be found that will show an increase in heart disease among the elderly.

I use a statin, and there is evidence that it will help me far outlive my grandfather, who died around 60. After his first and only heart attack, he languished in the hospital for eight days before dying. Nothing could be done for him back in the 1960s. Since then, there have been incredible advancements in preventing and treating heart disease. Today, heart surgeons are beginning to replace heart valves with minimally invasive surgery where equipment enters through a person's arm. Some life-saving heart surgeries are outpatient procedures.

The fear mongering is not limited to allegations that our health care system is in crisis. It includes dire warnings that pollution, hunger, and crime in America have been steadily increasing for decades, even on a per capita basis. The truth is that they have been improving. Our people were not born frightened of the world. They have been driven to their timidity by years of "doom and gloom" teaching.

At the beginning of the semester, I often tell my students that the only reason for them to be in my class is for them to change. This is obvious, but it surprises them. I try to ensure the students that change comes from more than simply learning some formulas, procedures, and tools. I hope my teaching changes the way they think so that they start to think based on reason and evidence. I hope they will search for their errors rather than confirmation of their prior beliefs. I tell them the primary reason individuals change their beliefs is when they become uncomfortable with their existing beliefs. I see part of my role as a teacher as helping them become uncomfortable with their current view of financial economics, and I cherish those times when students have challenged me and changed my conclusions.

Clear and objective thinking are casualties of the cultural war in America. The intelligentsia are trying to change America. To change America, they must make Americans unhappy with the current social system. The intellectual and political elitists want to make America's youth ashamed of being American. Our students are being taught that America is bad and that Americans are headed for terrible disasters unless they make drastic changes. Most dangerously, students are being taught not to allow others to speak if those people disagree with the intelligentsia. The intelligentsia know they cannot compete on a level playing field of rational discourse, so they are preventing speech on campuses that opposes their dogma and encouraging other students to do the same, even if it means initiating violence.

61. CAPITAL: THE INVISIBLE INPUT

I HAVE LED SEMINARS ABOUT economics in tall skyscrapers with large windows through which we could look out and see new skyscrapers being built. What goes into ensuring the successful completion of these marvelous projects? While most people see concrete, steel, and workers performing the work, I also see capital doing its job. For every nail, window, beam, and door that goes into that building, people had to invest their money in the project while taking the risk that they could get little or nothing in return. Capital is essential to a modern economy.

I dislike the term capitalism because it encompasses economies that practice crony capitalism rather than economic liberty and free markets. Crony capitalism occurs when business leaders or community organizers get government to use its force to benefit them by infringing on the rights of others. Crony capitalism prevents a level playing field.

Socialists dislike the private ownership and private control of large assets that occur in a capitalist society. But the deeper issue with most socialists is that they dislike the idea that people who have accumulated capital are able to earn additional profits by investing that capital. Socialists tend to view earning interest or profits on capital as being paid for doing nothing. They somehow believe that the people who save their money and invest in long-term assets such as buildings and equipment, or who invest in the stocks and bonds that fund those assets, do not deserve to be compensated for their sacrifice and for bearing risks.

I cannot understand how anybody would think that investors should invest and take the inherent financial risks without being rewarded with a higher expected return. Who would risk their money in the stock market if they knew they could get the same expected return (with less risk) from putting their money in the bank? Who would invest any money without expecting a profit?

Diehard socialists believe assets should be funded and owned by the entire society. But that system has not worked. When everybody owns an asset, nobody takes care of it. And, with economic production becoming more complicated and rapidly changing, true socialism is becoming more and more anachronistic. Many socialists hate capitalism because they have not saved their money and therefore do not have a lot of capital. Socialists want to control assets without having to make the personal sacrifices necessary to create the assets.

Capital is a massive but invisible factor in an economy's ability to produce goods and services. The people who provide capital need to be compensated. To people who think providers of capital are overpaid, I have one simple piece of advice: save up your money and become an investor. That we all have that choice is one of the great attractions of a free market over a socialist economy.

62. FREE MARKETS AND THE US HEALTH CARE SYSTEM

WHILE AMERICA'S HEALTH CARE SYSTEM treats traumas and diseases with world-leading quality, its finances are a mess. Hospitals in major urban areas are bankrupted or otherwise hobbled by massive demand for their services that generate costs that outpace their revenues. Patients face complex and seemingly unnecessary hurdles in trying to navigate the world of medical insurance. Many people defer medical care when their deductibles have not been met and accelerate care after their deductibles have been met. Some people go on medical spending sprees in December to avoid losing their health savings account dollars. Stories abound of treatment methods and location choices being driven by insurance companies rather than doctors and patients.

The political and intellectual elites place the blame squarely on America's free market system. They claim Canada and other nations that have adopted government-funded universal health care coverage offer better services at lower prices.

I have had in-depth talks with Canadians and Europeans about what really happens when medicine is socialized. It is true that routine care is often quite convenient, but the whole picture is not pretty. I listened to an Irishman recall his great suffering while awaiting heart surgery until a dear friend, who happened to be a cardiovascular surgeon, offered him free and immediate treatment in another country. I know Canadians who believe pets in Canada receive prompter medical attention than humans. Wealthy Canadians cross the border into the US to pay for timelier medical care. Socialized medicine has more problems than simply high taxes, but the elitists do not want Americans to know the truth.

The financial problems with the American health care system are not caused by free markets but by the opposite: government rules and subsidies. In America, the government requires hospitals with emergency care facilities to treat all patients regardless of their ability to pay. The result is that these high-cost emergency facilities are filled with drug addicts seeking fixes, homeless people avoiding the cold, and uninsured locals with trivial injuries or illnesses.

But the biggest problem is that the income tax system provides a huge tax break to workers with health care plans by making the employer's contribution free of income taxes and Social Security taxes. This provides a tremendous incentive for employee compensation to be made in the form of medical insurance rather than higher wages. This is the underlying cause of our health care system's financial problems; tax rules put the finances of our health care in the hands of our employers and governments, rather than letting us make our own decisions with our own money.

Years ago, medical insurance was inexpensive and was only designed for large expenses. It was called hospitalization insurance. Most insurance plans did not pay for small expenses such as visits to doctors and prescriptions. But medical insurance quickly expanded and became involved in virtually every medical service. The premiums paid for health care plans and the prices charged for medical care and pharmaceuticals correspondingly soared.

Most people do not think our health care financing problems are the result of government rules and taxation. Let's consider a thought experiment. Imagine that Congress passed legislation permitting corporations to include restaurant meal plans as employee benefits using money that is deductible for tax purposes, just like with medical insurance. The restaurant meal plans would work just like health care plans. If you are hungry, go to the restaurant of your choice and eat however much you desire in return for a minor co-pay after your deductible is met. And one more thing: let's assume that, if you do not have a restaurant meal plan, the government requires the restaurants to feed you even if you cannot pay for the food.

What would happen to our restaurant industry? First, restaurants would be overwhelmed with customers because their meal plans would pay most of the cost. And, if they had no meal plan, the restaurant would have to feed them anyway. Customers would not know or care how much each meal cost since they would pay little or nothing. Lobster tails for everyone? Sure! Restaurants charging exorbitant prices? You bet. So the government would have to step in to set food restaurant prices and control people's access to meals they deem unnecessary.

Restaurants near areas with high unemployment would be financially devastated by the requirement that they feed the unemployed for free. The government would need to provide massive subsidies to restaurants in areas with poor economic conditions.

The point is that the health care payment mess is not caused by the intrinsic nature of caring for one's health, nor is it caused by the evils of free markets. It is caused by government regulations and tax laws. Any industry would suffer the same problems as the health care industry if the industry was subject to the same public policies as the health care industry.

Another problem that emerges when government takes over an economic sector is that everyone begins to believe they have a right to receive full services. Americans increasingly assert a right to the highest quality health care regardless of their employment status or financial situation. And Americans increasingly believe the same should be true of higher education, childcare, and food.

My parents both worked hard to ensure they could pay for my brother and me to go to college. Would they have both worked so hard if it didn't improve their lives or the lives of their children? The astounding fact is that I was never able to attend a private school in my entire life because my parents worked so hard. Had they simply earned less and made sure not to save money, I could have attended an Ivy League school for free. Instead, every school I attended from kindergarten through my PhD program was public.

Perverse incentives like this are dangerous to a society. A society needs to be very careful when it tinkers with incentives. The long-term effects of distorting natural incentives will inevitably be devastating. And those effects emerge even quicker when a population is large and culturally diverse because perverse economic behaviors in large populations are not reined in by feelings of community.

I have asked my students what path their lives would take if America guaranteed that every adult and child would receive the same education, health care, food, clothing, public transportation, shelter, and was guaranteed a minimum income for the remainder of their lives irrespective of their decisions regarding education and work. Most students acknowledge that their choices in general, and career path in particular (if they chose one) would be substantially altered. And all students admit they would not be sitting in my class another minute if the incentives to do so disappeared. In the long run, the system would fall apart because there wouldn't be enough people willing to do the work that would keep such a foolish system going. Just ask the Venezuelans.

63. THE PEOPLE BEHIND THE CORPORATIONS

COLLEGE-LEVEL ECONOMICS COURSES AND TEXTBOOKS have one thing in common: they focus on producers as firms and consumers as people. But firms do not really produce goods—people do. Firms, like IBM and Uber are legal constructs, not people. I never saw IBM or Uber take a lunch break or mistreat a person. IBM and Uber are simply concepts that allow people to do things (including, at times, mistreating other people). IBM, Uber, and every other corporation serve as legal frameworks within which many types of people serve as producers: laborers, managers, providers of capital, lawyers, accountants, and so forth.

A firm is a collection of people who use various assets, such as buildings and equipment, to produce goods and services. But, in modern economics classes, the firm is viewed as an economic player that uses labor and raw materials to maximize profits. That allows economists to view free enterprise as a political battle between people and firms rather than seeing both consumers and producers as people. In recent years, this alleged battle between people and firms has increasingly served as the foundation for inciting class warfare over income inequality. Law firms claim to represent the people—implying that the people are in a fight against non-people. Who can people start economic battles with other than people, dogs? Every dollar won or lost in litigation and every dollar taxed and spent is ultimately a cash flow between people. Unions, corporations, governments, nonprofits, partnerships, sole proprietorships, and marriages are simply legal concepts that connect people.

In economics, the consumers are given names like Tom and Susan. Producers are simply called firms. A small amount of classroom time is spent assuming there are numerous firms competing on a level playing field to produce goods and services with greater and greater efficiency. But most classroom time is spent on the evils of firms and the damage they do to people. Economists obsess about monopolies, duopolies, oligopolies, and market failures, along with the need for government to solve all the problems. Of course, government is the biggest monopoly, but the political elites tend to run government, and so they approve.

Interestingly, economists see people managing the two sides of their economic lives (producing and consuming) when they analyze highly simplified scenarios with only two people (in a miniature economy) who gather and consume fruit and fish and where no capital assets are necessary. But, the people engaged in production in these simplified scenarios turn from Dr. Jekyll to Mr. Hyde when they become large firms and bring in capital. In truth, firms are contractual arrangements that bring diverse types of people and resources together with the desire to be more productive.

A movement that wishes to marginalize people begins by labeling them in a way that is dehumanizing. In an economics course the consumers are praised, as they should be, for their efforts to derive as much utility as possible while spending the least money possible. Consumers are praised for banding together to form co-ops and searching for lower prices. Laborers are praised for improving their lives by forming unions. But, by subsuming them under the label "the firm," society dehumanizes managers and the providers of capital and villainizes them whenever they seek to improve their lives. The goal is clear: dehumanize capitalists so elites can oversee the collective.

64. THE COSTS OF PROTECTIONISM

MANY YEARS AGO, I BECAME co-owner of a small sub shop. I was convinced that I could use the shop as a prototype for a successful franchise. I was wrong. It was a fiasco, an expensive fiasco. But it taught me several important things.

First, it gave me a lot of respect for successful entrepreneurs. Sure, some entrepreneurs are mostly lucky to be in the right place at the right time. But most entrepreneurs become successful by being much better at forming and running a business than I was. It usually takes incredible skill, focus, and hard work to be a successful business owner. I fear powerful politicians who never had a serious job in the private sector. They cannot understand what it takes to create value through voluntary commerce.

Another thing the sub shop taught me was that the key to making the sub shop profitable was being efficient at producing a desirable product.

There's a lesson there regarding international trade. Politicians tell us we need to expand our exports by subsidizing them and minimize our imports by taxing them because exports create jobs and imports destroy jobs. But our politicians are short-sighted. When we subsidize our corporations to enable them to sell their products abroad, and when we protect them from foreign competitors, we are harming American efficiency and productivity. It's the opposite principle that a successful sub shop owner operates on.

The reason any particular American company has no exports is that its costs of making and shipping its product exceed the amount of money it can get paid. For example, I might have a company that takes leather and labor and makes shoes. But, with the high cost of labor in the United States, I could not possibly compete with firms from developing nations that have labor costs 90 percent lower than mine. American taxpayers working in jobs that make economic sense should not subsidize my shoe exports.

Taxing imports comes with the same problems as subsidizing exports. Rather than subsidizing my American shoe firm to promote exports, America can impose tariffs on shoes from other countries to discourage imports. The result is the same as with subsidies: an inefficient industry is kept on life support. In this case, the bill is being paid by American shoe consumers.

In effect, governments that subsidize exports or tax imports punish their efficient producers with taxes and reward their inefficient producers. Do we really want to keep our most inefficient industries on life support at the expense of profitable firms?

Politicians somehow think subsidies by foreign nations of their industries hurt us. Let's take that argument to the extreme. Imagine if all the other nations in the world subsidized their exports to the point that Americans could buy cars, computers, clothes, and lots of other stuff at ridiculously low prices. We would be able to live like kings by focusing our energies on those industries where we are the world's most efficient producers.

People my age remember the pathetic quality of domestic cars relative to foreign cars in the 1970s. Our domestic manufacturers had been protected from competition for decades. Then the inevitable had happened: our firms became more and more inefficient, and domestic cars became less and less competitive.

A country that taxes imports and subsidizes exports is like a professor that gives Fs to students with the highest exam scores and As to students that have the lowest scores. It is a recipe for long-term failure. Similarly, protectionism can destroy the very prosperity it was intended to protect.

65. GOVERNMENTS AND ORGANIZED CRIME

I TEACH FINANCE COURSES, AND a lot of students take the course because they want to get great jobs that pay well. I have no problem with that because I believe that people who improve their lives through cooperation in a free market help make society better.

However, there are two primary ways to gain wealth, and only one of them is noble. The noble way is to create value. In a free economy, everyone can take part in creating wealth, be it as an entrepreneur, a manager, or an entry-level worker. Creating wealth or value means producing output that has a higher market value than the inputs used. Many people create value: laborers, managers, clerks, entrepreneurs, investors, to name a few. People who create wealth are justified in gaining some or even all that wealth.

But, there is a sneaky and destructive way to gain wealth, and that is to connive to take it from someone else. That is the purview of common criminals, crooked businesses, organized crime, corrupt governments, and corrupt labor unions.

Too many people carefully observe the world, looking for where wealth is being created so they can figure out a way to steal it. We know this is true of common criminals. They spend a lot of time casing a joint or a neighborhood looking for pockets of wealth and an opportunity to spring into action and take what does not belong to them.

The same approach is practiced on a large scale by crooked organizations. These organizations study where the wealth is and figure out a way to steal a share. We all get the emails and phone calls from various businesses trying to scam us with Ponzi schemes or blatant fraud. When law enforcement cracks down on them in one area, they move to another.

Organized crime steals a lot of money a similar way: they find out which businesses are making good money, and then they hold those businesses hostage to their violence. The successful business owners find themselves forced to pay outrageous fees for garbage removal or protection they do not want.

Governments do the same thing. They find successful organizations and then go after them. The federal government levies windfall profits against them or fines them for one thing or another. State governments launch investigations and attack the wealthiest firms until they agree to pay fines. Local governments levy massive real estate tax rates and utility rates against the most profitable organizations.

Labor unions can do the same thing. Unions watch a firm grow until it reaches a highly profitable size and then attack the firm to transfer its profits into the pockets of their members and leaders. I have no objection to workers going on strike. The problem is when unions use federal labor laws written by politicians (in exchange for union support) that force firms to negotiate under conditions imposed by the government, or when unions exercise coercion to block non-union employees from serving as replacement workers.

Many community organizers are also guilty when they approach successful organizations (i.e., deep pockets) and threaten lawsuits and blockades unless the organization pays them off.

Have you ever thought about how much of our time and money is wasted trying to prevent thieves from taking our stuff? Think of the wasted productivity spent on locks, keys, passwords, protective software, safes, guards, vaults, security cameras, theft detection devices, fortifications, and justice systems just because some people prefer to steal rather than create value. Imagine what the world would be like if everyone stopped using coercion or fraud to take other people's stuff. All those efforts to take stuff and protect stuff could be diverted into making more stuff for everyone.

66. Trends on Starvation

I LIKE TO ASK YOUNG adults a simple question: is human starvation a problem that is getting better, getting worse, or roughly staying the same? I find it amazing that most young people have been indoctrinated with a doom-and-gloom view of modern society to the extent that they honestly believe starvation is an increasing problem in the world. Nothing could be further from the truth.

Throughout recorded history, human starvation and death hastened by poor nutrition has been the rule rather than the exception. Human life expectancy did not reach forty years until the first decade of the 19th century and it has doubled since then. Most of the world could not even expect to live beyond age thirty prior to the 1800s.

In the last two centuries, world population has exploded. Until the last 200 years, in most societies most of the time, starvation was a fact of life. Turn now to the US where, in recent decades, death by starvation has been entirely avoidable. If someone is found to have starved to death in the US today, police will most likely investigate what caused him or her to starve. Prisoners threaten to starve themselves and hunger strikes appear in national headlines as we panic over how to get these people to start eating. And obesity, not lack of food, is the big problem (pun intended), especially among the poor! How lucky we are.

In the 1960s, my mother would admonish me to eat all the food on my plate because kids were starving in India, China, or Africa. While pockets of food shortage persist, most deaths by starvation have been wiped out. Death by starvation is increasingly rare in China and India. So there was nothing inherent about India or China that necessitated starvation. But starvation and malnutrition have been stubborn issues in sub-Saharan Africa. What is it that causes sub-Saharan Africa to continue to struggle so disproportionately? Are the people there stupid? Are they lazy? Does God not love them? I believe most of the explanation is captured in a single word: "institutions." Important institutions are lacking, along with the rule of law, private property rights, the freedom to trade, and reliable law enforcement and judicial systems. Could the persistent problems in some regions of the world be caused primarily by poor institutions in need of reform? Could aid be delaying the necessary reforms? An unbiased view of the world's economies makes it abundantly clear that long-term malnutrition persists only in some regions, regions that have received massive aid packages for decades and have not improved their institutions.

67. GOVERNMENT PROGRAMS AND INFLATION

YEARS AGO, WHILE TEACHING IN Greece, I became friends with a Greek man who made his fortune from a flawed Greek government program. The Greek government attempted to attract US dollars to their country by offering to use drachmas to buy US dollars from its citizens at an exchange rate that greatly favored the citizen relative to the market exchange rate. Perhaps the idea was that its citizens would bring more US dollars into the country that way. The man who made his fortune off the program knew many Americans. When they visited Greece, he would meet them at the airport and offer to exchange drachmas for their dollars at the market rate. He would turn over the dollars through the government's program to obtain drachmas at the government-subsidized rate and pocket a handsome profit. The net result was that wealth was transferred from the public coffers to his pocket with no added dollars brought into the economy.

I observed lots of behavior in Greece that involved manipulating government economic policies to make personal gains at the expense of net societal losses. America is headed down that path because, as government becomes more powerful at all levels, entrepreneurial efforts will be increasingly driven by gaming government programs and policies rather than by meeting consumer demand. This means people will grab for bigger pieces of the pie, but the pie will be getting smaller. Most will be worse off.

The most economically dangerous thing government can do is interfere with market prices. In doing so, the government distorts the signals communicated throughout our economy by prices. When governments interfere in markets, people increasingly evaluate the benefits and costs of their decisions by the prices set by government bureaucrats rather than the prices that would have been set purely by supply and demand in a free marketplace.

In 1971, the United States began a plunge into full-blown socialism. Inflation had reached five percent per year, and the economy was not doing well. Government had caused the inflation problem by expanding the money supply. Nevertheless, it was time for them to fix it. But, instead of correcting the monetary policy (which they did not do until October 1979), Nixon tried coercion. On August 15, 1971, Nixon addressed the nation about inflation:

"The time has come for decisive action—action that will break the vicious circle of spiraling prices and costs.

I am today ordering a freeze on all prices and wages through-out the United States for a period of 90 days. In addition, I call upon corporations to extend the wage-price freeze to all dividends.

I have today appointed a Cost of Living Council within the government. I have directed this council to work with lead-ers of labor and business to set up the proper mechanism for achieving continued price and wage stability after the 90-day freeze is over."

Yes, the United States was headed for full government control of prices and wages. My understanding is that rationing tickets were being prepared to meet the inevitable shortages. Think of the dis-connect: government increases the money supply and then blames laborers and businesses for raising prices and wages to adjust. The government takes over private decision-making, having completely messed up their role in government functions, such as creating a stable money supply.

Thankfully, support for the price controls fizzled. But the idea is back on the table again as federal bureaucrats insert themselves even further into our lives with the increasing cooperation of the judiciary, legislature, and media. If the bureaucrats get full control over our wages and prices, our economy will begin a Venezuela-like decline, and our entrepreneurs will begin to act like my friend in Greece. Incentives matter.

68. SUNK COSTS AND OPPORTUNITY COSTS

TWO OF THE MOST IMPORTANT lessons in economics are to ignore sunk costs and include opportunity costs. Sunk costs are expenses that have already been paid and therefore are irrelevant to all future decisions. Human nature often leads us into allocating too much time and energy toward making up for past mistakes.

For example, suppose someone owns a very high-mileage used car and recently put $2,000 into repairing body damage to it from an accident. The person then finds out there is a mechanical problem requiring $2,000 worth of work. If fully repaired, the car would probably be worth about $2,500. However, assume the car could be sold now for $1,000 to a scrap dealer. An economist would conclude that the car should be sold for scrap. In fact, the economist would also note that the decision to fix the body damage was a mistake. But the person who recently put $2,000 into bodywork on the car might well decide to sink another $2,000 into the car by authorizing the mechanical work. The reason is that scrapping the car may cause emotional pain to the owner from acknowledging that the $2,000 of bodywork was a mistake. But, to the extent that people can think rationally, the best course of action is to maximize future satisfaction, not dwell on the past.

Opportunity costs are losses from events that do not occur. Opportunity costs are often ignored at great financial peril. For example, I often see landlords who let rental properties remain vacant for years. The landlord ignores the tens of thousands of dollars of rental income being lost. The landlord does not see these losses; therefore, they are easy to ignore. I often ask these owners how they would react if someone came to the door of their house and demanded $100 in cash each day unless a particular problem got solved. Of course, they would drop everything and try to solve the problem. Yet, when they lose $100 each day in lost rent, they tend to be complacent.

Let's apply the concepts of sunk costs and opportunity costs to a nation's economic and governmental growth.

Economic freedom unleashes the natural desire of people to create innovative solutions to the problems we face. To the extent that a society taxes, regulates, restricts, and litigates against its citizens when they pursue their chosen economic activities, the society is burdening itself with enormous opportunity costs. The innovative solutions don't come to pass. But activities not undertaken are opportunity costs and are invisible. The society will never know what it missed.

When a society diminishes incentives to innovate, it misses opportunities no one can even imagine. No one was able to predict what the internet has done, and no one can predict what the internet won't be able to do if people are prevented from creating, failing, and offending.

As a society, we should learn from sunk costs and then forget about them. Unfortunately, America keeps throwing more and more dollars at failed programs in the apparent hope that eventually they will succeed. Examples include government give-away programs. The list is long: cash for clunkers (intended to get old automobiles off the road), checks to everyone to stimulate the economy during recessions, huge checks to purchase electric cars, huge checks to fund solar panels, and numerous income tax credits. Our politicians keep dreaming up and implementing huge give-away programs in the hope that they will find something effective. But the benefits are never worth the costs.

Consider our federal and state programs, initially designed to provide temporary safety nets for the truly impoverished. They have turned into multi-generational giveaways. Taken together, all levels of government in the United States are approaching annual expenditures of a trillion dollars per year on welfare payments and other cash distributions, health care subsidies, food stamps, child care, educational subsidies, tax credits, and other programs combined. Have these programs worked? Have these programs lowered the number of people needing long-term assistance? No. Dependency on these programs as a whole is higher than ever. Perhaps Americans are reluctant to admit these past failures because it is so painful to admit that so many of these costs have become sunk costs.

69. Rights as the Border between Legal and Illegal Harm

Asking my students what it means to have the right to freedom of speech tends to stimulate a great discussion. They typically answer that it means a person can say anything they want as long as it doesn't hurt someone.

But people don't need to be protected from saying something that doesn't hurt or annoy someone else. All day long, we interact with others in ways that offend or harm others. Our speech offends, our looks offend, our religious beliefs offend, and our actions cause harm. We harm people by what we do and by what we leave undone. We harm others, albeit mostly in minor ways, in traffic, in elevators, in business offices, and in gyms.

Rights allow us to function by protecting people from being responsible for saying or doing things that do hurt other people, especially powerful people. Within certain limits, the right to free speech, in particular, allows people to hurt or annoy other people. More broadly, rights allow citizens to pursue their own happiness, even when that means hurting or annoying other people.

Of course, there are limits to our natural rights. But the limits to one person's rights are determined by another person's rights, not the other person's opinions, preferences, privileges, or expressed levels of hurt. We have the right to attack the privileges of other people, even government officials. But we do not have the right to infringe on the natural rights of other people because, although our rights are more important than other people's privileges, they are not more important than other people's equal rights. Rights define the accepted and unaccepted behaviors within our society. Our country was founded on this idea.

Put differently, rights form the lines between controversial behavior society allows and controversial behavior society does not allow. Rights are safe harbors within which we can enjoy our liberty, even when other people don't like it.

Our right to free speech, in particular, allows us to say anything without legal repercussion, as long we don't infringe on the rights of others, with certain exceptions. So we can say hurtful things such as "I think that Jimbo is a fool," since Jimbo does not have a right to be free from other people's expression of negative opinions. It should not matter how much our opinions hurt Jimbo. Perhaps Jimbo's wife will leave him, his employer will fire him, and his dog will no longer like him as a result of hearing our opinion that Jimbo is a fool. But it is our right to express that opinion and not his right to prevent our free speech.

On the other hand, think of the many things freedom of speech does not protect. We cannot slander or libel Jimbo. In other words, we are not free to broadcast a harmful fact about Jimbo that is untrue (for example, saying Jimbo is a sex offender). But we are free to express an opinion. We also cannot threaten Jimbo with aggression. And we cannot make a verbal contract with Jimbo and then renege on the contract claiming free speech.

Why can't we do these things? Because they deny Jimbo the natural rights to life, liberty and the pursuit of happiness. Jimbo's rights are as important under the law as yours, mine and everyone else's.

Aside from those few exceptions, people should be free to say—and do—almost anything. But America has lost sight of what it means to live in a free society. Alleged victims are successfully suing people and especially businesses over any hurtful speech and hurtful actions, regardless of whether the supposed victim had any of his or her natural rights violated. Our rights are increasingly being violated in order to acquiesce to the privileges of others.

70. BORN IN THE USA

I OFTEN ASK STUDENTS TO list the consumer technologies since 1850 that most changed the day-to-day lives of people in the developed world. Here is a typical list: automobiles, televisions, electric refrigeration and air conditioning, radios (broadcast and two-way), photography (still and motion), sound recording, light bulbs, computers, the internet, airplanes, antibiotics, phones, birth control, and food storage.

I then ask them if the list teaches us about how technologies are developed or how they become available to ordinary consumers. In other words, are there common links in the creation or spread of these technologies that would help us understand what it takes to develop and popularize these technologies?

A Harvard student at a seminar I led once responded that the common link was that they were primarily "developed with direct help from government." I asked what sort of government support the Wright brothers, Thomas Edison, George Eastman, Alexander Graham Bell, and Clarence Birdseye received. His reply was only to claim that the government should get credit for creating the internet. Al Gore and I would disagree with him. But his opinion indicates the extent to which people see what they want to see and disregard the rest. It also confirms the old saying, "You can always tell a Harvard man, but you cannot tell him much."

The intelligentsia believe what they want to believe. They can always find at least one example that supports their position, even if the preponderance of the evidence refutes it. If you try to point this out to the intelligentsia, they will simply change the subject. The intelligentsia do not genuinely want to learn; they want to teach. They believe they already possess enough knowledge to manage everyone's lives better than they're being individually managed.

Most discussions about this list of technologies lead the students to think about who was behind these changes. The discussions lead to three primary observations. First, the major leaps in advancing these technologies were performed by individuals, not bureaucratic organizations. Second, most of those individuals were residing in the US when they developed the technology. Third, most of these technologies, if not developed solely by Americans, were at least popularized first in the US.

Why has the US served as the birthplace of so many world-changing advances? Is it because Americans are more intelligent, stronger, harder working, or luckier? I believe it is because of America's institutions—primarily economic freedom, but also its system of law and justice, its heritage of individuality and responsibility, its support of private property rights, and its goal of treating everyone equally under the law.

I believe America's long-term history of success in economic innovation is also attributable to its personal and political freedoms. In his book, *A Time for Truth*, William E. Simon writes *that "political freedom and economic freedom are inexorably linked." The more I have studied economics, the more I have come to agree with Simon's assertion. Economic creativity and financial courage are stifled when people are politically and personally oppressed.*

I have met bright and hard-working students from all over the world. But, generally, they tend to lack the path-breaking creativity that less-skilled Americans seem to possess. I attribute a good part of this creativity to the American culture that has bred confidence in the importance of the individual and encourages them to challenge the assertions of their leaders and teachers.

71. IS THERE ANY SUCH THING AS TOO MUCH LOBSTER?

I ASK MY STUDENTS WHY most of them like lobster tails more than an ordinary fish, such as whitefish. Their answer is always something like this: lobster is sweeter and has great texture. In an important sense, they are wrong. The correct answer is we prefer lobster to whitefish because it costs more. If the price of lobster suddenly and permanently fell to ten cents per pound, two things would happen. First, a lot of people would eat a lot of lobster at a lot of meals. Second, people would eventually get sick of eating lobster. It's human nature. Economists call it declining marginal utility. People buy the least expensive items that bring them pleasure until they tire of those items and become willing to pay more to enjoy a wider variety of items.

The human body is amazing. The evolution of life forms from primitive organisms to seeing, thinking, and feeling human beings based, apparently, on nothing more than randomness and natural selection, is mind-blowing. The fact that all of the information necessary to build a human body can be contained in a microscopic strand of DNA is just as fascinating.

The evolution of organisms and market economies is very similar.

Economies have developed from primitive and limited markets for basic goods into sophisticated networks that organize a multitude of independent workers and guide them to meet the needs of a multitude of consumers. It is especially amazing to me how such economies communicate the necessary information about all those needs and capabilities through a simple set of market prices of various goods and services.

Organizing production and communicating information about needs centers on prices for oil, wheat, copper, cotton, plywood, beef, gold, milk, electricity, etc. Market prices that orchestrate an economy include two of the most important, but most often overlooked prices in a society: interest rates (the price of money through time) and risk premiums (the prices required to get someone to bear risk). Prices are the constantly evolving strands of DNA that communicate the information necessary for a society to reach its highest goals.

The market prices of lobster, whitefish, and other seafood serve as a guiding star to communicate priorities to every fisherman, every wholesaler of seafood, every consumer of seafood, and everyone who uses seafood in prepared foods.

For example, if the market price of flounder is three times the price of whitefish, every fisherman is motivated to work three times harder to catch a pound of flounder. Consumers select flounder only when they perceive three or more times enjoyment from eating flounder. Food manufacturers, from cat food producers to chowder producers, select flounder only when they perceive three or more times the benefit of using flounder rather than whitefish.

Market prices guide everyone toward cooperating with their fellow humans in every facet of their lives. They create prosperity and guide a rapidly changing economy. But market prices have a big image problem. People hate the message that market prices send them every day. Market prices tell us that the things we most like to do (for example, take walks, relax, watch TV, or listen to music) pay us little or no money. Conversely, the things we least like to do (for example, work as Arctic fishermen) pay the most. Prices signal to us what a well-functioning economy needs, but they constrain us from enjoying the good life without having to meet the demands of others. Let's not shoot the messenger—the price system—just because sometimes we do not like to hear the truth.

72. FINANCIAL MARKETS AND CASINOS

I INTRODUCE THE TOPIC OF market efficiency to my students by asking two questions. First, does it make more sense to invest in a firm with solid and growing earnings or a firm with declining sales, profits, and market share? It seems a no-brainer that investors tend to do better with firms that have been successful and well managed.

My second question: if you were betting on sports in Las Vegas, would it make more sense to bet on a highly ranked team with a great win-loss record or a weak team with a terrible win-loss record?

Some students give the same answer: go with the better track record. But some students come alive, especially those who appeared to be asleep in the back row. "Not so fast," they say. They claim it's not clear which team is the better bet, because the odds or point spreads at the casino—the price of a bet, in other words—adjust such that the bets tend to be equally attractive.

If these students are right, and I believe they are, then shouldn't the same logic have us conclude that the market prices of stocks adjust to make each investment equally attractive?

Scholarly literature suggests the answer is yes. Many scholars have researched which stocks are more attractive than others. In general, they conclude that market prices of investments continually adjust to drive prices toward levels where the investments are equally attractive.

Market efficiency is the idea that competition drives financial market prices toward values that fully reflect the prospects for each investment. Although no market is perfectly efficient, major financial markets are efficient enough that it's extremely difficult to gain an edge by trying to buy underpriced securities and sell overpriced securities. We can trust that, when people use market prices to inform them of the benefits and costs of a decision, they're using the most accurate valuations known by anyone.

It's hard for most people to accept that, in financial markets, only a few exceptional people can find consistently underpriced securities. My students, for example, enter my course believing that by reading a few books and analyzing a few companies they can make better investment decisions. They believe this because thoughtful analysis does guide them to make many decisions better. Diligent research can reveal which college to attend, which house to buy, which airplane ticket to buy, and which job to take.

But financial markets are different. I point out to my students that financial advisors who claim to have the ability to do the research and analysis to consistently beat the market almost certainly do not have that ability. If I had the ability to consistently pick winning stocks, I would keep my mouth shut rather than ruin my bets by cluing in others. I would buy a tropical island. I would relax on the beach, surrounded by all the people I love, and write postcards to my relatives.

73. Organizations Not Worth Dying For

THE WORLD HEALTH ORGANIZATION ESTIMATES that nearly six million children under the age of five die each year due to "conditions that could be prevented or treated with access to simple, affordable interventions" like vaccination and adequate nutrition. That averages out to about 16,000 young children per day. I point out to my students that, as painful as it might be for them to listen to my one-hour lectures, on average more than 600 children under the age of five die from easily preventable causes during each one.

How can there be such enormous differences between the abilities of different cultures and regions of the world to provide health care and other good things? How can these differences persist for decades? What can be done about it? Are NGOs (non-governmental organizations) the answer?

The United Nations thinks NGOs are the answer. It established UNICEF as an emergency fund in 1946 to provide health care to children in countries devastated by World War II. UNICEF stands for the United Nations International Children Emergency Fund. As with most aid organizations, the size of its budget and its bureaucracy became a major goal—and so its mission has changed to suit that goal. By the 1970s, UNICEF was persistently providing food and other aid directly to the impoverished residents of Africa. The word "emergency" in the original name of UNICEF is telling because the word refers to situations that are unexpected or unforeseen. Can anyone seriously contend that the need for most of the services now provided by UNICEF is unexpected?

UNICEF has changed its name simply to the United Nations Children's Fund, and its budget has soared from less than $1 billion per year twenty years ago to more than $5 billion per year recently.

And it evolved from its emergency footing to a focus on long-term child development and then to a comprehensive view of the child as "a future agent for economic and social change." But there is little reason to think it has made progress in its stated goals, despite the increase in money and staff.

One of the most telling signs of a dysfunctional society is when it rewards destructive behavior and punishes edifying behavior. The sad fact is that most governments and NGOs are better able to grow and prosper when they are incompetent and ineffective. In other words, when NGOs solve problems, the need for the NGO often goes away. But if the NGO fails to solve a problem—or makes it worse—the perceived need for the NGO grows, along with its budget and power.

When a corporation makes products that are inferior to the products of its competitors, it tends to shrink and fail. When a governmental agency or NGO fails in its mission, it usually is able to demand greater resources.

Fifty years ago, I saw images of starving children in Africa. They continue to starve. Yet the organizations that were funded to solve these problems starting in the 1960s and 1970s are bigger and more powerful than ever, with few accomplishments to boast about. Why do we continue to take this approach? As is often said, insanity is doing the same thing over and over and expecting things to come out differently.

74. FREE TO CHOOSE COMMUNAL LIVING

I AM NOT OPPOSED TO voluntary communal living. There are times and places for everything under the sun, and socialism is no exception. How do we distinguish between socialist ideas that work and those that don't? I do that by observing the outcomes.

Some degree of communal living enhances our marriages, families, and friendships. Because we are reared in highly socialized living arrangements, even as adults, many Americans want to impose socialism on others. When should socialism be imposed, and when should economic freedom be allowed? The best answer is that every adult should be allowed to make his or her own decision to live free or join communal arrangements.

American politicians do not accept that answer. They are attacking the right of citizens to govern their own lives. The leaders of this war on our natural rights are the self-crowned emperors of the nanny state.

Michael Bloomberg, former mayor of New York City, is a case in point. He and other politicians from the New York City area have led efforts to use government to tell people what they can and cannot eat, what they can and cannot do, and even what they can and cannot say. They are being championed by the media, by the intellectual elitists, and by the masses that receive their living by having the government take money from the rich and give it to them.

Why are we bowing down to these new emperors of the nanny state? Prior to the 18th century, royalty was typically understood to be speaking the word of God. Royalty was assumed to have God-ordained rights to control the lives of others. A small band of bright and innovative 17th- and 18th-century thinkers somehow were able to shed the shackles of traditional thinking and conceive the notions that people should be treated equally under the law, that they have the right to govern their own lives, and that they deserve liberty. America has been the crowning glory of their miraculous insights.

America is an economic miracle. But most Americans do not really know how an economy works or understand what America did to become so successful. I would never think of going up to a well-trained scientist, musician, historian, or engineer and attempt to explain to them the intricacies of their specialty. However, often after I tell someone I am a finance professor, they tell me how financial markets work and how to invest my money.

Most politicians know nothing about businesses and financial markets. They do not understand how free economies self-organize and how they convey information quickly and accurately through market prices. Yet our workplaces are becoming increasingly government-controlled. Politicians attack market wages for being unequal, and they increasingly call for wage equality (in the private sector only, of course). I think of the world my grandchildren will inherit, a world in which the emperors and advocates of the nanny state will micromanage more and more of their economic lives.

The solution is to let each adult select the level of socialism or communal living they wish for themselves. If you wish, join a commune, favor products made by socialists, hire socialists as workers, and choose them as friends. But America should continue to be a place where people can also opt out of socialism.

75. THE RIGHT TO NOT EMPLOY

I LIVED IN A BIG union town—Bethlehem, Pennsylvania—for more than twenty years. Bethlehem Steel shut down its massive factories and declared bankruptcy shortly after I arrived. No, I didn't cause it. Decades of poor management and powerful unions did.

Unionization itself is consistent with economic liberty. If two or more workers, or even all workers, wish to unite to negotiate with management or to go on strike, it is their natural right.

The problem arises when government sides with unions by trampling on the natural rights of the business owners and the workers who would replace the strikers. Historians recount the major violent labor disputes of the late 19th century and early 20th century as if corporate bosses ordered private and public police to violate the natural rights of striking workers. Did corporate bosses order the police to hunt down the striking workers, drag them out of their houses, and beat them for not working? No. People have a right to choose not to work.

Most violent labor disputes occurred when union members used force to oppose the right of business owners to hire non-unionized labor and the right of non-unionized labor to go to work for business owners who were trying to hire them. The violence occurred primarily because the striking workers tried to prevent new non-union employees from working in the factories. Nothing is a more egregious violation of natural rights than to use violence to prevent a citizen from going to work. And the violence interferes with the natural right of employers to hire other workers when their existing employees refuse to work.

Unions should be proud when workers peacefully unite to squeeze employers into offering better contracts. But leftist historians and union advocates go too far when they portray the history of labor disputes as dominated by the initiation of violence by business owners against peaceful union members. When union members, or anyone else, deliberately interfere with the natural rights of business owners by attacking scabs and blocking factory entrances, it is they who are the initiators of violence, and it is the business owners and replacement workers who have the right to defend themselves, their property, and their natural rights.

America today faces a problem with unionization of government workers. There is a massive public sector (federal, state, and local) in which politicians and bureaucrats negotiate with their unions while the taxpayers pick up the bill. The problem is not unionization. The problem is the mixing of two monopolies: government and unions.

Politicians and unions can scratch each other's backs. The politicians approve expensive contracts knowing that the money costs them nothing; it is paid for by taxpayers. The unions make donations to the politicians and organize voter support for the politicians using union dues. The two monopolies feed each other at taxpayer expense. The result is that pension liabilities and health care costs of federal governments, state governments, municipal governments, school districts, and various transportation authorities have exploded.

Many unionized government employees can pad their pensions by working (or supposedly working) enormous amounts of overtime during the years immediately before retiring. The pension is based on the average wages of the last few years on the job. So some middle-aged employees can retire with generous life-time pensions that taxpayers must fund for the remainder of the retirees' lives—forty years or more. Municipalities and school districts are being bankrupted by some of these plans. Healthy, middle-aged, government employees are often able to retire with huge life-long pensions and medical insurance. Their communities are being crushed by massive tax increases.

The problem is well described as crony unionism, partnerships of unions and government designed to fleece taxpayers. It is nearly as bad as the crony capitalism practiced by big corporations.

76. Getting to Know All about You

For many years, my mother served as the director of volunteers at the community hospital in a somewhat small town. It seemed like my mother knew everyone. My mother was an extrovert. She loved meeting new people and seeing people she already knew, and she loved talking. By knowing so many people, including all the hospital's volunteers, she was able to run a smooth and effective program for many years. Her ability to connect with so many volunteers allowed her to be accepted as the program's leader.

But the hospital's program was relatively small. Managing very large groups of people requires a different approach to leadership. Communal living also requires leadership that knows much about everyone in the commune because there is a limit to the number of people with whom anyone can maintain long-term and reasonably close ties. An anthropologist named Robin Dunbar estimated the number to be around 150 people. I believe that Dunbar's number roughly indicates the highest population size a commune can healthfully sustain.

A commune requires cooperation among its members to be successful. But cooperation becomes more difficult as the size of a community increases. As a commune becomes larger, each member has less affinity for the others and more relationships become strained. A commune needs leaders with the authority to settle disputes. But how can the leadership of a very large community understand the needs and abilities of all its members? How can people be sensitive to the preferences of others when nobody in the community knows more than a small percentage of the other members? How can members understand other members when they have never met most of them? When resources become strained and difficult decisions need to be made, some members will inevitably see their lives negatively affected by other members with whom they have no close personal connection.

How, then, do any communistic regimes survive? The answer is: by force. They must prevent their more successful members from leaving the country. Large communes need central planners who ensure pigs are being slopped, lettuce is being planted, and fields are being fertilized. As the size of the group grows, as personal relationships get diluted and, as the knowledge required to coordinate all the economic activities and connections becomes exponentially larger, cooperation must yield to coercion. Nobody volunteers to slop the pigs. Assigning the worst chores to those who express dissent is a good way to get all the chores done while affirming the power of the leadership.

These concepts regarding truly communal arrangements apply to a lesser degree to moderately socialist economies. Socialist economies function better when people share similarities, such as ethnicity and religion. They also function well when their institutions regarding law, justice, and education are strong. Socialist economies function best when they emerge from a market economy based on private property rights and a strong work ethic. Sweden used to be an example of a moderately socialist economy that thrived with a relatively homogenous population and a heritage based on private property rights and hard work. But, absent those conditions, socialism inevitably unravels if people are free to exit. I have visited several of Europe's other socialist economies a few times and have been amazed by the shabby and aged condition of so many of the buildings, the difficulty of getting business done, and the lack of discretionary income. Those economies are suffering from decades of socialism's perverse incentives.

So how can large free-market economies thrive without a central leader that knows everyone? The answer is two-fold.

First, the primary economic role of the government in a free market economy is limited to protecting the natural rights of its citizens. In a rights-based society, the leadership does not decide which farmers grow which products and how. Government can be effective in this limited role: executing a straightforward mandate to protect private property rights and other natural rights.

Second, free markets allow the economy to self-organize. Important information about resources, technology, and consumer preferences is quickly communicated throughout the economy by market prices. A market-based economy does not require leadership that knows everything, knows everybody, and micromanages everyone. Free markets thrive because individuals with access to markets and market prices tend to be better managers of their own lives than government committees located in distant capitals. Efficient behavior is rewarded by the market and inefficient behavior is punished by the market. This means a lot of elitists don't like free markets.

77. Paying Boxers More than CEOs

Students are attracted to sensational urban legends, especially those about the failures of our economic system. One widespread example is the myth that CEOs in certain industries such as the automotive industry have been withholding dramatic improvements (e.g., fuel efficiency) from the market for many years because they are colluding with producers in another industry (e.g., oil) that would lose profits if the technology were adopted.

Common sense debunks this myth. More than 25 automotive companies worldwide each make more than one million cars annually, generating annual revenues exceeding $20 billion at each of the 25 firms. With this much money at stake and this many firms competing for market share, how could a breakthrough technology be kept secret through the collusion of every company?

Let's turn to another frequent criticism. Students complain about the outrageous salaries of corporate executives. I agree that some highly paid corporate executives are probably not worth their salaries, especially those earning tens of millions of dollars per year for running firms with mediocre performance. But that statement is even more true of professional athletes, popular musicians, and movie stars. How many major league pitchers earn millions of dollars annually yet post losing records? In 2016, more than a dozen celebrities and athletes made at least $65 million. Only two corporate executives took home $65 million or more that same year. The most famous boxers, like Floyd Mayweather, earn nearly $100 million in a good year. Does anyone honestly think boxing is more important to society than running a $500-billion firm employing hundreds of thousands of workers?

Yet I hear students lambast obscene corporate executive compensation over and over, while I almost never hear them complain about what professional entertainers are being paid. Simple analysis shows why a superstar entertainer can command a salary approaching $100 million per year. We see and understand what most entertainers do to earn their money, and we realize they really are producing great value. When billions of people worldwide pay for movies, songs, or live sporting events, the value the entertainer creates can soar into the billions of dollars.

Why do young people appear to enjoy spreading misinformation about corporate greed and maligning corporate executives for their high pay? More generally, why do some students appear to want to believe the economic system is rigged? And it is not just young people. Many people spread stories about corporate greed, corporate arrogance, and the failures—false and real—of a free market economic system.

The answer is easy. We don't like the feedback we get from a free market economic system in the form of prices and wages. We all seek great deals and free lunches, but competitive markets tend to eliminate them. The best cars and vacations cost lots of money. The most fun college courses often lead to the lowest-paying careers. The jobs we most desire are scarce or don't pay well. These realities are painful, but they simply reflect the realities of supply and demand. Painful as it is to admit, some corporate executives truly add value to a corporation and have skills that few of us have. Just as painful is admitting that our cherished criticisms of corporate conspiracies have no foundation and are mere myths.

78. MODERN-DAY LUDDITES

AN AGE-OLD BATTLE BEING WAGED throughout the world concerns the false belief that technology slashes employment. Yes, new technologies destroy old jobs. But that's good because it creates newer and better opportunities. As I write this, the US unemployment rate is at a historic low of less than 4.0% at the same time that the application of technology is at an all-time high. Except for recessions or depressions, 5.0 percent has been the average unemployment rate over the last 125 years. So it is clear that long-term technological growth has not led to high unemployment.

In the last 150 years, advances in technology led to improvements in productivity that enabled the US to decrease the percentage of the workforce in agriculture from over 50 percent to about 2 percent. But the reduction did not cause mass unemployment. It enabled growth in new areas. This has been the long-term pattern: obsolete jobs are replaced by an equal number of new jobs. Nevertheless, famous leftist economists mysteriously agree that "this time" things will be different and there will be massive unemployment. These elitist economists tout new economic policies by claiming that they will prevent massive unemployment (if administered by them).

Think how much technology has changed due to electricity, cars, computers, phones, and television. Think about how many jobs have been destroyed in agriculture, mining, and trades. Yet new jobs keep being created while the economy thrives, and the technology drives our population to ever higher levels of wealth. And along with that wealth has come abundant food, better health care, a cleaner environment, more travel, and better entertainment.

In economics, those who argue that technological innovation should be stopped are labeled Luddites, especially when the argument is made based on the belief that technology causes higher long-term unemployment. The original Luddites were a group of English textile workers in the early 1800s who protested the use of mechanical innovations that were threatening their employment. Some Luddites went so far as to destroy the textile equipment. The jobs that are destroyed by new technologies tend to be more back-breaking and boring than the jobs being created. And, there can be no doubt that the entire population from poorest to richest enjoys dramatically higher standards of living now compared to a century ago.

Especially in the years since the financial crisis of 2007-2008, I have noticed increasing ignorance in young people about the benefits of technological advances and economic prosperity. Many of them are convinced that organic foods have led to better health, that GMO foods have been proven dangerous, that the quality of health care in the US has declined, that air pollution and water pollution in the US are worsening, and that chemicals in our environment are destroying our health and reducing our longevity. Their fears are based on myths. Yet no amount of logical reasoning or scientific evidence can dissuade this new brood of Luddites. They believe their lives would be far better if they could reverse the technologies of the last 125 years and return to the happier times of the 19th century. If young people do not wake up to the economic realities, they might begin to reverse the progress of the last few centuries and end up needing to get up at 6:00 a.m. every day to work in the candle factories. If, like in the 19th century, 50 percent of them are forced into old-fashioned agricultural work, there will be a lot of unhappy millennials. Worse yet, their decision to reverse modern economic ways could jeopardize the greatest Ponzi scheme that's ever existed—Social Security—just about the time I plan to cash in.

79. Libertarian Principles

Through the years, one of the steadiest trends in the political knowledge base of my students upon entering my class is their increasing awareness of libertarianism. Thirty years ago, perhaps one percent of my students in each class had some familiarity with the term. Now, most do. However, they increasingly lack the foundation on which to understand the implications of libertarian ideals because their understanding of the founding principles of the American Revolution declines with each class.

Libertarianism is the view that the primary role of governments should be to protect the rights of individuals to life, liberty and the pursuit of happiness, including the right to benefit from the fruits of their labor, trade, and capital. Libertarians also support civil liberties such as freedom to practice a religion, exercise a sexual preference, and engage in free speech. Libertarians believe people are born with these natural rights—that governments do not bestow these rights.

Students are becoming more aware of libertarian viewpoints on "hot" public policy issues, but they struggle to accept expanded liberties, perhaps because they have been raised by parents who protectively hover over them and because they have government officials who have created a protective "nanny state." Students in recent years are increasingly fearful, especially of taking unsupervised risks.

I also struggled with libertarian principles when I first heard them. My immediate reaction was to question how society could function and be protected if government did not exert widespread control over actions such as drug use, prostitution, and gambling. I wondered what would happen to our society without extensive labor laws, antitrust laws, pharmaceutical controls, consumer protection, safety standards, etc.

The academic discipline of finance tends to attract—or perhaps even create—libertarians. Several of my colleagues in finance took the time to explore and discuss my concerns. I learned that many of society's challenges can be solved without government intervention, often through market mechanisms.

Despite what extreme libertarians say, libertarianism is not perfect, and it can never prevent or solve all problems. But it does better than any other system, and that is the appropriate standard. Other things are incredibly successful but imperfect. The 1998 New York Yankees compiled a stunning regular-season record of 114 wins against only 48 losses and went on to sweep the World Series after winning 7 of 9 games in the American League playoffs. Many baseball fans believed this team was the best they had seen in at least 40 years.

But the 1998 Yankees had 1,025 strikeouts at bat, committed 98 errors, allowed 156 home runs and gave up 466 walks. Similarly, libertarianism does not create a perfect society. But it is the most libertarian nations that thrive and lead the world in both economic and cultural aspects. The successes of societies based most heavily on libertarian principles contrast starkly with the outcomes of societies that pursue extreme socialism.

Authoritarian societies tend to languish. America is becoming more and more authoritarian. A friend of mine who is an elementary teacher in an urban area tightly controlled by a centralized school system has been instructed in her public school to refer to all her students as friends rather than boys and girls. Teachers in public schools are increasingly told exactly what to teach and how to teach it. Government's increasing control of what our children are taught is the worst form of authoritarianism because the things the government is increasingly controlling are the minds of our children.

80. PRICES AS OUR GUIDING LIGHTS

EACH DAY, FROM THE MOMENT we wake until we fall asleep, our lives are a series of analyses, decisions, and actions. Rational decision-making means evaluating benefits and costs and accepting only those decisions that we perceive as having greater benefits than costs. How do we evaluate the myriad combinations of benefits and costs we confront every day? Successful people in thriving economies make decisions based on market prices.

In recent years, to communicate this point, I have begun semesters telling my students that the first things I do every morning are to get out of bed, go to the bathroom, urinate, flush the toilet, and eat breakfast. How do market prices guide the way I start my day? For starters, I own a house with an indoor bathroom. My decision to buy a house with a bathroom was guided by my salary—the price of my labor—and the price of a house with a bathroom. More immediately, the toilet in my house uses quite a bit of water in disposing of the urine, a fact driven by the near-zero price of water and the fact that urine has a negative price (I'm willing to pay to get rid of it). And when I eat breakfast, I am careful not to waste orange juice because it is expensive. Prices guide us throughout the day, whether we think about them consciously or subconsciously.

Let's turn from how prices guide our decisions to how much information those prices convey. Most people, even well-trained economists, think the reasons for the levels of most market prices are somewhat obvious. It seems obvious that water should have a lower price than orange juice. But prices are driven by incredibly complex factors.

It is not obvious why water should be so cheap. The price of water reflects knowledge of what resources it takes to construct and maintain a reservoir, make pipes, and then dig tunnels for those pipes and lay and maintain them. The price incorporates the cost of chemically treating water, including the cost of making and transporting the chemicals. There are also the costs of pumping the water, metering the water, billing for the water, and administering the water utility. Each of those component costs require a host of inputs that must be priced. For example, the cost of a pipe is driven by the costs of labor, ore, trucks to ship the ore, fuel to heat the ore, machinery to form the pipes, and so forth. Looking into the cost of the trucks to ship the ore means looking into the inputs for manufacturing trucks, and so it continues.

How can a single person know the value of this endless series of inputs that go into an item as seemingly simple to produce and transport as water? They can't. No single person or government committee can understand all the costs that underlie a product in a modern economy. They need market prices to fill in the information they are missing.

Let's turn to the fact that the market price of urine is negative—in other words, I'm willing to pay to have it taken away. Urine's lack of market value tells us that not one of the billions of people on this planet has been able to find a wide-scale, commercially viable use for urine that makes it worthwhile to collect it. I do not need to be a biologist or chemist or entrepreneur to know this; I just need to know that all the wisdom of the world that's relevant to my decision-making can be signaled in a single price.

Market prices constitute a system of lighthouses helping everyone navigate an increasingly complex and rapidly changing world in their many intricate decisions. Market prices are miraculous in quickly and accurately reflecting the changing economic realities of our world. To me, the price of my house, the price of water, and even the implicit price of urine conveys their value (or lack of value) and the value of the things that go into them. And, like everyone else, I respond by deciding what to economize on and by how much. Economically successful people harness the power of the information revealed in market prices. In fact, we all benefit when the entire society uses market prices to make wise decisions.

81. Stealing from the Rich and Giving It to the Intelligentsia

Utility is an economic term for happiness. Economists often assert that the objective of a person is to maximize their utility over their expected lifetime. So a crucial issue in modeling economic behavior is to find the relationship between wealth and happiness.

The traditional assumption is that people are happier at high levels of wealth than at low levels of wealth. Economists also assume a person with $2.5 million is only modestly happier than a person with $1.5 million, while a person with $1.5 million is substantially happier than a person with only $0.5 million. The technical jargon for this is that the utility from wealth increases at a decreasing rate—also known as diminishing marginal utility.

These assumptions make a lot of sense. Maslow's hierarchy of needs and other psychological theories point out that people can rank their preferences from the things they consider most important (food, clothing, and shelter) to those things that are less important (imported food, designer clothes, and second homes). This means the utility of each person from wealth increases at a decreasing rate. A person with this utility function views increases in his or her wealth as less important the richer he or she becomes.

Many economists use this assumed property of utility functions to argue that, as a result, it makes sense to tax wealth from the rich and to give it to the poor. The logic is that the benefit gained from giving $100 to the poor person outweighs the harm done from taking $100 from a rich person.

The error is that, even if everyone's marginal utility diminishes with wealth, it does not mean that $100 means more to a poor person than to a rich person, any more than it means that an ice cream cone means more to a skinny person than it does to a fat person. To the contrary, I observe many more obese people than thin people anxiously waiting in line for ice cream.

The famous movie *Citizen Kane* has as its premise the idea that even small amounts of money can mean a great deal to a rich person, while *It's a Wonderful Life* portrays the willingness of people with modest means to help a person in need.

The argument that the aggregated happiness of the entire society increases when wealth is transferred from the rich to the poor relies on the assumption that the utility functions of all people are very similar. But this ignores the truth that Hemingway noted, that the rich "are different from you and me."

The intelligentsia believe they know more than we do and that is why they should rule society. They oppose people who became rich from commerce and wish to redistribute the wealth of the bourgeoisie to the poor. The biggest problem with wealth redistribution is that stealing from the rich to give to the poor reduces the size of the pie by distorting natural incentives. People produce less and spend more energy trying to game the political system. Societies that go down that path, like Venezuela, stunt their growth and development. But the intelligentsia do not see it as theft. As Reagan noted, "We have so many people who can't see a fat man standing beside a thin one without coming to the conclusion the fat man got that way by taking advantage of the thin one."

82. Trends in American Influence Peddling

People are increasingly trying to persuade, control, and even force others to alter their behavior, especially regarding economic matters. Every person's business has become the business of every other person. When an airline or fast-food company mistreats a customer, it becomes national headline news and that customer heads to court for another multi-million-dollar award. But, when customers steal from a business or employees are negligent in performing their duties, the elitists call for leniency and government protections.

We seem to be spending a lot of time trying to coerce others to do things that annoy us less and serve us better. We would be better off minding our own business. Minding our own business means protecting our own natural rights and respecting the natural rights of others.

The intelligentsia in general and elitist economists in particular are unabashed in their efforts to engineer a better society. They urge government to tax or outlaw the things they dislike and subsidize the things they do like. They are zealous in their attempts to indoctrinate others with their politically correct views through government-funded programs such as public television, but make sure opposing views are not even allowed to be presented. The intelligentsia ridicules and attacks those who dare challenge them with labels such as racist, sexist, and homophobic.

When persuasion fails, the intellectual and political elitists "take the gloves off" and turn to coercion. For example, the intelligentsia believe fast food is bad. So, in many cities, they pass laws preventing entrepreneurs from opening chain restaurants. They call for taxes on soda drinks and outlaw them from schools. They lobby government to reward and punish at their behest. The lifeblood of modern economics, as preached by the intellectual elites, consists of using taxation and subsidies to guide people's choices in politically correct directions: tax junk food, subsidize art. Tax value creators, subsidize the jobless. Tax big business, subsidize cultural enterprises and other non-profits.

But consider the hypocrisy. When a corporation uses advertising to encourage consumption of their product, the intellectuals howl at the immorality of trying to alter people's natural choices. Yet most of the economic policies espoused by the intelligentsia call for government to use taxation, subsidies, and regulations to do exactly the same thing: alter people's natural choices. Economists call for government to force people to transform their lifestyles in the directions favored by the elites. They believe government force should be used to eliminate tobacco and junk food while subsidizing fresh vegetables. They believe corporations' advertising should be tightly controlled because it distorts people's natural preferences. But they want government to use taxes to pay for advertisements and educational programs that promote their messages, which are equally designed to distort people's natural preferences. Have you noticed how many billboards are government-funded messages?

The implicit belief of the intellectual and political elitists is that their motives are altruistic while the motives of corporations are evil. Why should we think the elitists and so-called public servants who run our government are more noble than our corporate leaders?

Market forces tend to discipline corporations more than they discipline government. When a corporation advertises products that consumers try but dislike, consumers punish the corporation by lowering their trust regarding their products and adverting tactics. Corporations marketing poor products tend to experience diminished revenues and influence. But government's power to tax and spend is not so easily diminished.

83. THE POVERTY OF NATIONS

WHY DO SOME NATIONS PROSPER and others languish? One explanation is that the rules for social interaction we learn as children don't work well when applied to commerce involving millions of adults.

Baby birds learn one set of behaviors in a nest where they are helpless and they need benevolent parents but, eventually, the young birds must learn to fend for themselves in a world full of threats and opportunities. Rules outside the nest differ from rules inside the nest.

Analogously, optimal human behavior in small groups such as families is very different from optimal behavior in a marketplace. It is the job of parents to force healthy behavior on their children. But should the intellectual elite serve as nannies to the adults in a large and modern economy?

Our youth are increasingly being raised in parent-controlled bubbles. Few children nowadays experience the freedom of a childhood in which they play without adult interference. Further, our society increasingly believes government should micromanage our lives as adults. The result is the emergence of the nanny state.

Another factor that determines whether a nation prospers or languishes is whether the government protects the natural rights of people to create and enjoy wealth. Prosperity in a modern economy requires a strong government with stable and effective institutions, including an effective legal system. But it also requires that this strong government does not stray into social engineering and micromanagement. It is a tough balancing act that depends on deep-rooted beliefs in the right of the people to liberty.

Nations languish when government takes wealth from those who created it and gives it to others (or permit others to directly take wealth from those who created it). This is exactly what America is increasingly doing. Governments tax the very things that make a nation prosper: the creation and preservation of wealth. They tax wage income, business income, investment income, real estate, sales, and consumption. They then give this wealth to those who do not work and do not save. In the long run, it is unsustainable and devastating.

84. Birds Do It, Bees Do It, and So Can Most People

I SPEND A LOT OF time observing birds. I find their ability to care for themselves fascinating. Who is it that ensures birds serve their long-term best interests by building nests, caring for their young, and making the long, arduous journeys south in the winter and north in the summer? Is it the role of big government agencies or local volunteers? Who guides these birds?

Of course, nobody needs to do anything to get birds to behave rationally. They have a natural drive to pursue their self-interest both in the short term and the long term. They do not need a government of birds, and they certainly do not need people. Animals have natural instincts to care for themselves and their offspring; if they did not, they would be extinct.

The ability of animals to care for themselves in nature is so clear that most people today are adamant that we should not interfere with the natural habits and habitats of these creatures. But all this good sense gets thrown out when we think about human needs rather than animal needs.

How is it that our human societies have evolved to the point where we think the vast majority of humans need constant penalties and rewards orchestrated by governments to be functional? Are people dumber than birds?

Many see society as having the moral obligation and practical need to provide emergency health care, free education, free childcare, free breakfasts, free lunches, food vouchers, welfare, housing, counseling, and even cell phones to poor people. On the other side, they say it is necessary to punish people for making decisions that the intelligentsia believe to be poor, such as smoking, drinking, taking drugs, gambling, and not having health insurance.

We have ended up as a society where, in many places, it is a crime to feed wildlife and a crime not to pay taxes designed to feed poor people—a portion of whom simply refuse to work when they can receive food and health care for free.

85. FEEDING THE NEEDY

I OFTEN PUT THE FOLLOWING statement in front of my students on a PowerPoint slide:

> *I believe it is wrong to feed a poor person. Feeding a poor person creates dependency and diminishes the poor person's dignity. My motto is "Do not feed a poor person."*

I ask my students to speculate who would make this statement. Would the person be more likely to be a liberal or a conservative, a rich person or a poor person, and so forth? The consensus is that the person is likely old, white, male, and conservative. And most students think the speaker must be quite hateful.

I then change the words "poor person" to "bear."

I believe it is wrong to feed a bear. Feeding a bear creates dependency and diminishes the bear's dignity. My motto is "Do not feed a bear."

I ask the students to speculate what type of people would make the new statement. Most students believe it is no longer clear this statement would be primarily made by a particular type of person. Some argue the statement is more likely than not to be made by a young liberal—someone who tends to be more aware of how people's interference with nature causes destruction. Generally, the students agree with the statement.

Next, I change the word "bear" to "duck."

I believe it is wrong to feed a duck. Feeding a duck creates dependency and diminishes the duck's dignity. My motto is "Do not feed a duck."

Most students disagree with the principle when applied to ducks, but they think it is silly rather than hateful. Most agree that feeding a duck is harmless.

Finally, I ask why their attitudes change so much when they consider the same belief applied to three different contexts: humans, bears, and ducks. They generally conclude that our attitude toward charity depends on our view of people. If we view people like bears, we are reluctant to extend charity. Bears are strong. Bears are most noble when they fend for themselves. If we view humans as somewhat helpless, like ducks, we extend the charity freely.

When I see a homeless person begging for money on a city street, I almost never help them. I do not think I care less than others who do help. But I see giving them money as encouraging them to continue on a path that harms themselves and others. I fear some people give money to the homeless to feel they have done something wonderful for a person weaker than themselves. As the great 20th century author Ayn Rand said, "helping a person can be immoral, robbing them of something that matters a great deal—being able to say, 'I did it, I provided for myself'." Rand also notes how abhorrent it is when people help the poor to receive a feeling of self-esteem or even superiority.

86. PROGRESSIVE CRONY CAPITALISM

ONCE MY STUDENTS HEAR ABOUT my fondness for free markets, they often assume I am a conservative who supports big business and thinks government should help big corporations. But I hate crony capitalism in all its forms. In crony capitalism, business and political leaders are in cahoots with each other. Crony capitalism is an enemy of free markets, economic liberty, and long-term economic growth.

Crony capitalism will exist whenever government leaders are allowed to use their power in ways that deny citizens their natural rights. And the more powerful the government is, the more crony capitalism there will be. While the rest of the country has its economic ups and downs, Washington, DC seems to get bigger and bigger. Thousands of huge office buildings now surround the epicenter of the federal government. These buildings are visible evidence of the extent to which big corporations and other special interests are vying to curry favor with and procure benefits from the federal government.

There has been a big change in crony capitalism in the last few decades. Most high-level government officials have become smart enough to keep their crony arrangements legal. Most do not receive cash bribes while in office. The game is played this way: government officials spend their time building government power. Big US corporations, and even some foreign governments, develop reputations for being generous by paying lavish consulting fees and speaking fees to our retired government officials. Before retirement, our high-level officials favor the big corporations and foreign governments, knowing they will soon be receiving hefty fees. The corporations signal their willingness to continue playing the game by making sure already retired officials receive lucrative engagements. For example, most of our former presidents cash in big from speaking engagements—to the tune of millions of dollars.

Crony capitalism is not just for big business. Crony capitalism is any attempt of business managers or business owners to curry special favor with governments. At the federal level, crony capitalism involves big corporations. At the local level, crony capitalism usually takes the form of local business owners trying to keep large, successful corporations from operating in their locality. Examples are actions to keep national chains such as Home Depot, Walmart, and McDonald's from "destroying their community." But the real damage national retailers do is to the local business owners—not the community at large. It is the established wealthy and elite who benefit when they prevent new businesses from entering a market. It is ordinary citizens who suffer from being unable to patronize new businesses.

Elitists are increasingly becoming crony capitalists at the local level. Federal-level crony capitalism is with big firms. Local-level crony capitalism is when elitists use local governments to benefit small, inefficient businesses.

87. LIARS, DAMN LIARS, AND POLITICIANS

DECADES AGO, THEN-FIRST LADY HILLARY Clinton led a failed effort to change the health care system. At the time, I attended a meeting with a congressman and politely asked him why he thought he had any moral right to support Clinton's proposed coercive legislation that imposed tight restrictions on the relationships between doctors, patients, and insurance companies. He must have been caught up in the power of Washington, DC because he viewed the question as loony. He claimed the legislation wasn't coercive. Years later, his ideas triumphed: Obamacare passed. Soon it was no longer a citizen's right not to buy government-prescribed health insurance. In forcing every citizen's participation in government-mandated health care plans, our government had inextricably inserted bureaucrats into our personal health care decisions.

Some people mask their beliefs from others by using deceptive terms. They use convoluted language to obfuscate the real issues and to sabotage attempts at constructive dialogue. How can we work together with mutual trust when some people are avoiding a healthy discussion of issues?

Years ago, Senator Harry Reid set a new standard for avoiding honest discussion. The setting was an interview with talk show host Jan Helfeld in which Helfeld asked the senator to justify the use of taxpayer money to fund give-away programs such as welfare. Helfeld wanted to know how Senator Reid could explain why the government is justified in robbing Peter to pay Paul. Reid duplicitously argued that the government does not force people to pay their income taxes. He proclaimed that the income tax system is "voluntary."

Under pressure to justify his absurd proclamation, Senator Reid eventually explained that taxpayers can choose whether their tax payments will be withheld from their paycheck or paid directly. He also pointed out that citizens can avoid some of the income tax by taking advantage of tax deductions and tax credits. Senator Reid is not stupid; rather, he aimed to mislead. The discussion establishes one of two things. Either Senator Reid was so caught up in a zealous mission to tax and spend that his common sense was distorted, or he has no interest in a frank discussion of the morality of taking money from persons who earned it and giving it to people who did not.

Harry Reid's outrageous responses to Jan Helfeld can be easily located on the web, and I recommend readers of this book to listen to them. Our taxes paid the salary of this arrogant and disingenuous man. Even politicians of this type—and most are of this type—refer to themselves as "public servants." In truth, they view citizens as their servants, not their peers. How else could they lie to us in their attempts to justify coercive taxes and regulations like Obamacare?

88. Searching Voting Booths for Escaped Convicts

MOST STUDENTS TODAY ARE NOT well educated about our society's institutions. Consider the following sentences: *Guns constitute a real danger to innocent people. Guns should be eliminated.* Many of my students agree with eliminating private ownership of firearms.

Let's repeat those sentences while changing one word: *Bees constitute a real danger to innocent people. Bees should be eliminated.*

Bee stings kill almost 100 Americans each year, according to the National Institute for Occupational Safety and Health. Millions more are inconvenienced by nonfatal stings or by the need to keep medical injection kits at hand. But no one is calling for the elimination of all bees. While we recognize that bees are vital contributors to agriculture through pollination, is there any analogous benefit from guns? That is where a huge divide occurs in America, with some believing gun ownership protects America from tyranny and others seeing virtually no benefits from private gun ownership.

The issue comes down to rights. Natural rights protect activities that people cherish, but that sometimes inconveniences or harms others. Everyone wants to be able to exercise the rights that he or she cherishes. But, when a person exercises a right, it often offends or harms other people. That's the whole point of rights: protecting people who do things that—at times—offend some other people. The second purpose of rights is to protect people from harm that may be caused by the exercise of lesser rights by other people.

The intelligentsia and political elitists advocate voting rights. They are outraged that convicted felons lose their right to vote even after they have served their time in prison. They argue that felons deserve the ability to help select our country's path and that we should show them our confidence in their ability to make wise decisions. However, these same elitists believe that the felons should never be allowed to own a gun again. Apparently, the intelligentsia and political elitists believe they should be allowed to determine who does and does not have various constitutional rights.

The Founding Fathers included gun ownership as a constitutionally protected right. They explicitly demanded this right for militias. We do not need militias to hunt. Militias and, more generally, Americans' right to own guns is to protect people from other people—especially tyrants.

An honest and proper way to seek to eliminate gun ownership by ordinary citizens is a constitutional amendment. But the intelligentsia and political elitists know such a constitutional amendment has no chance of passing soon. So, in complete disregard for the Constitution, they seek to eliminate constitutional protection of private gun ownership through local legislatures and activist judiciaries. They are tearing down one of the foremost institutions that made this country great—the preeminence of the Constitution and the rule of law—by using liberal judges to legislate from the bench.

With such people trying to gain control over our lives in direct violation of the Constitution, it is hardly surprising that many other people are loath to give up their guns.

89. Y2K AND THE SCOURGE OF CHANGE

TECHNOLOGY IS THE PRIMARY REASON that human life expectancies have almost doubled in the last 200 years. But new technology can appear scary.

I vividly remember the countdown to the new millennium. Fear mongers were forecasting an apocalypse when our computers' calendars turned from 1999 to 2000, causing computers with only two spaces reserved to hold the number of years to crash. The fear mongers forecasted gloom and doom and called for government intervention. I was spending several days per week consulting at a major bank in Manhattan in 1998 and 1999. I noticed a huge "war room" at the bank filled with people busily going through the firm's software to prevent disaster. I relaxed when I noticed that their work was finished almost a year ahead of time.

Many people prepared for the New Year's Day of January 2000 by hoarding cash (because ATMs were forecast not to work) and toilet paper (because the cash registers at stores were forecast to fail). But self-interest prevailed and people with work that required computers took the necessary precautions to ensure their interests were protected.

I've lived near the Amish and, like many, I've enjoyed observing their bucolic way of life. The Amish people's refusal to adopt most modern technologies has preserved for them a lifestyle that, at times, appears quite inviting. But I wouldn't take such an invitation, and I certainly wouldn't wish for all of society to do so, either.

The Amish are reluctant to embrace new technologies. For some reason, they picked the late 19th century as the dividing line between technologies they would initially accept and "new" technologies they would often reject. The Amish have not rejected all technologies of the 20th and 21st centuries. Each Amish community decides whether to accept new technologies as they come along.

While not all Amish communities are alike, many have chosen to reject ownership of automobiles, phones, and 20th century machinery for noncommercial uses. Many Amish communities allow Amish businesses such as dairies to use electricity, phones, and other aids that help them be more efficient or, in some cases, help them meet government regulations. Many Amish communities allow their members to use the modern conveniences away from their businesses if those objects are owned and operated by others. In some Amish communities, the Amish refer to everyone else as "the English," regardless of their ethnic origins. And the Amish can, for example, ride in cars as long as they're owned and operated by "the English."

Many millennials in recent years have become increasingly antagonistic toward economic efficiency in much the same way that the Amish reject technological change. They feel we should return to the "good old days" by owning chickens and goats, replacing cars with bicycles, and tending large gardens to grow crops for our own consumption. They treasure products that are handcrafted using primitive techniques. They scorn the tendency of corporations to streamline production in a way that causes them to lay some workers off and reduce others to being cogs in a mass production machine. Of course, the more intellectual and elitist of these millennials want to impose these ideals on everyone, rather than simply practicing them in their own lives.

Should we freeze life with current technologies, or perhaps even return to the supposedly good old days of prior centuries? Observing the Amish only gives us a partial glimpse of what life would be like if these elitist millennials get their way. Would life a hundred years from now be just a little different from today? No, it would be severely changed—and for the worse! Existing technologies actually die when people lose freedom.

That aside, when a small group such as the Amish freeze their way of life, they generally don't try to prevent others from innovating. The Amish observe the innovations of "the English" and reap the rewards. The Amish can decide which new technologies to accept and which to reject. More important, the Amish benefit from the technologies of others even when they don't own and operate them. Many of the Amish travel great distances in cars owned by "the English," and they travel to modern hospitals for serious medical problems.

The Amish know what they're rejecting because they can observe the new technologies being adopted by the "English." This is key. If everyone stopped innovating, who knows what technologies we'd miss out on experiencing. Fifty years ago, nobody could imagine the things we enjoy today such as the internet, wireless devices that talk with us, and minimally invasive robotic surgery. My father worked in the television industry and helped usher in the age of color TV. But he could never have imagined that someday a 55" color TV would weigh less than 30 pounds and cost less than a single night's lodging in a big city. We should expect more such unpredictable wonders if we let entrepreneurs be free to innovate.

If the intelligentsia and political elitists had been victorious years ago in placing limits on innovation, what existing medical break-throughs would we have missed? And what unimaginable technologies would we miss in the future?

90. FOREIGN CARS WITH "BUY LOCAL" BUMPER STICKERS

COLLEGE TOWNS ARE FILLED WITH foreign-made cars proudly displaying *Buy Local* bumper stickers. Apparently, their drivers don't recognize the irony in their own actions.

When challenged, advocates of *Buy Local* claim the campaign is about advocating better nutrition by eating food that has been harvested recently. I have no problem with people being willing to pay more to buy locally grown produce if they believe it has been more recently harvested and might be better-tasting or more nutritious.

But doesn't the "better food" argument imply that the bumper sticker read: *Buy Fresh*? And why do these people feel they should preach to others about eating fresher food? I don't see bumper stickers that read: *Exercise Often, Floss Regularly, Wash Behind Your Ears*, or *Get Annual Checkups*. But I see lots and lots of *Buy Local* stickers.

Based on my conversations with *Buy Local* advocates, I think this is a campaign promoted by supporters of small-scale American farms. I ask my students whether they would stop preaching *Buy Local* if self-driving, electrically powered trucks could safely drive through the night to get produce from distant areas into our neighborhood by early in the morning—right after being picked. They say they wouldn't. It is not about freshness, transportation costs, traffic congestion, or pollution. It is a romantic fascination with small-scale farming.

The real motivation behind the *Buy Local* phenomenon is about turning the clock back to a time when people did business directly with each other and knew each other. It is a campaign against middlemen and large businesses. It is a campaign to support people they know and like: people more like them.

I like to ask students how they feel about a hypothetical bumper sticker that says *Buy White*. They are sickened at the thought, as they should be. But, when we choose to buy otherwise-equal goods at higher prices because we wish to bestow favor on one group of people (in this case local people like us) rather than other people (lower-cost producers), we are discriminating. Maybe to wealthy American Northeastern whites, their particular form of discrimination seems victimless. But I suspect that to the hard-working farmers and laborers in agricultural regions who are victims of *Buy Local*, the discrimination feels terrible, regardless of the motives.

One of the most precious ideas in our society is that the reward to producers should be based on the quality and value they can deliver to their customers rather than on the color of their skin, their connections to political power, or whether we like them. Favoring local producers is a step down a dangerous path. Competitive markets do not discriminate on the basis of anything other than quality and price—and that puts us all on an even playing field free of discrimination.

91. MILKING TECHNOLOGY

WHEN I WAS A LITTLE boy, I often visited a dairy farm belonging to my grandmother and her husband, Ben. I observed how hard Ben worked. Ben milked well over 20 cows twice per day by hand. His work also included feeding the cows, moving the cows from the barn to the pasture and back, cleaning out the barn, taking care of the fields and fences, and maintaining the buildings and equipment. My grandmother helped make ends meet by working full-time at a factory. Together, they worked a large garden. They had no central heat, no cable TV, no air conditioning, and only a single phone—on a busy and annoying telephone line that was shared by numerous nosy neighbors. These shared telephone lines were called "party lines." My students have a decidedly different understanding of what a "party line" is.

A lot has changed in a little over 50 years. On a modern dairy farm, the cows are milked in "milking parlors" enabling 12, 16 or even 24 cows to be machine-milked simultaneously. Only one or two workers are needed to clean the cows and attach the milking machines. They do their work from a pit that enables them to work standing up. Computers automatically keep track of the cows—each wearing electronic identification devices—so that the dairy's database is updated with milk production. In some cases, the computers monitor and manage the cows' food consumption cow by cow.

Let's look at the results. In a little over 50 years, the number of cows a single worker can manage has grown more than tenfold. On top of that, dairy cows today can produce three to four times as much milk as they did 50 years ago, thanks largely to better breeding and nutrition. The combination of better milking technology and better breeding is that the quantity of milk that can be generated each day by a single worker on a large dairy farm today is 30-40 times higher than it was 60-70 years ago on small farms.

Advances in food production such as dairy work mean our society can feed itself with 90 percent fewer workers today compared to a century ago. While almost half the workforce in 1900 was devoted to agriculture, about two percent was devoted to agriculture by the end of the 20th century.

Economic historians often measure economic prosperity of various societies by the height of their bodies. The reason is that wealth enhances nutrition, which in turn generates health and height. For example, the average height of European adult males has been estimated to have grown at almost one centimeter per decade during timespans in which their economies were healthy.

Throughout most of the world, food is becoming increasingly

affordable. The real price of eggs (i.e., the price adjusted for inflation) fell by over 80 percent during the 20th century in the United States. And, when food prices are measured in the length of time an average employee must work to afford a unit of food, the advances in efficiency are astonishing.

The bucolic vision of a person calmly milking a cow by hand lures today's youth into romanticizing the idea of having our society return to the happy days of simpler times. Visions of happy cows, happy workers, and more nutritious milk dance through their heads. Ben would have scoffed at the idea. He loved it when, in the 1960s, he could afford to convert to using milking machines. Ben would probably point out that few Americans know what it is like to literally work 365 days per year from dawn until dusk. I remember him telling me it had been decades since he was able to travel more than 40 or so miles from home due to the burden of getting his daily farm work done. I shudder to think of the consequences to our society if the do-gooders are able to impose their romantic fantasies on the rest of us. We would surely lose our ability to enjoy today's abundance while working a mere 40 hours per week.

92. Let them Eat Non-GMO, Organic, Gluten-free Bread

Most students—and many non-students—are convinced the US is experiencing a crisis of poverty in which a greater and greater proportion of our population is suffering more and more. This is not supported by the economic data. The poor today are not starving—they weigh more than the average person a century ago—and they receive better health care than anyone received a century ago. Most poor people in the US today live in climate-controlled homes and eat better-preserved foods, thanks to improved food storage and transportation. Many poor Americans today have lives that kings could not have hoped for centuries ago: enjoying the benefits of dental and medical advancements, great music, warm clothing, central heat, air conditioning, safe lighting, fresh foods, and relatively fast and safe transportation.

There can be no doubt that the poor among us have benefited from the economic growth and technological advances of recent centuries. But students are not taught to appreciate how our economic growth and advances have helped the poor. Rather, many academics try to convince their students that the living conditions of the poor are spiraling downward due to income inequality.

They also teach that poverty is forced on the powerless—deliberately or not—by the wealthiest one percent. They and non-academic intellectual elites claim that the wealthiest people's pursuit of wealth means the poor must eat unhealthy food, go without childcare, live on the streets or in substandard government housing, and drop out of school and start single-parent households. Some go so far as to claim that keeping vast numbers of citizens in poverty is the goal of the rich—that somehow having lots of poor and unemployed people in the US enables the richest citizens to be richer. All of this implies there's a fixed quantity of wealth to be divided among the people so, if millions of people can be made to get tiny shares, others will be able to grab large shares.

I have never met a wealthy person who thought they benefited from the unemployment of other Americans. The reason is simple: unemployment does not make the pie bigger. Everyone benefits when poor people develop skills, work, and get wealthier.

It is income inequality, not high unemployment, that play a healthy role in society. If all incomes were truly equal, few people would invest in acquiring high levels of education and skill or devote themselves to producing outstanding results. How many would work hard if they believed it would in no way improve their standard of living or the health and education of their children?

Poverty is not increasing, and the wealthy are not creating poverty. But these facts undermine policies focused on punishing the rich rather than rewarding the productive, the inventors, and the innovators. Policy makers are vilifying businesses and wealthy people to garner votes. We can do better. If America continues its current path, we will never know the tremendous value, innovations and inventions the world will miss from this misguided claim that wealth and income inequality cause long-term poverty.

93. A Wagon Worth Falling Off

FOR A VIVID ANALOGY OF a free society's transition to a welfare state, envision the society traveling on a long, hard journey that a few of its people are unable to navigate under their own power. A large group of people pull a wagon in which a small group of people sit because they are unable to walk on their own. Of course, in the analogy, the people pulling the wagon are the people in an economy working hard to earn a living while the people resting in the wagon are those on some type of welfare. I've heard this analogy mentioned by a few conservative politicians.

Obviously, some people really do need direct help from others. It is my experience that there are many people who are happy to help others who are truly in need. With many generous people and relatively few people in true need, the society should thrive.

But, what if some of the able-bodied people begin to see that riding in the wagon is easier than pulling it? What if these able-bodied individuals can feign back injuries or emotional disorders that cannot be verified for legitimacy? The first result, based on the simplest of economic principles, will be that there will be more people sitting in the wagon (being on welfare) and fewer pulling the wagon. But it gets worse. As the burden on the people pulling the wagon gets harder, animosity will build between the two groups and the problem will spiral out of control.

My wife and I love to watch birds. She fills a birdfeeder in our yard and, within days, many birds congregate around the feeder. The birds are fun to watch, but at times it gets discouraging to see them fight with each other so often. I see a lot of similarities in human behavior. Free stuff is attractive.

Note that every dollar received by someone who did not work for it must be paid by a person who did work for it. America is at a crucial fork in the road. One path leads to increased socialism, and the other returns America to the values that made it the world's economic leader.

Government cannot solve this problem by doing the same things on larger and larger scales. Each time government increases the number of welfare programs and makes them larger, the problem only gets worse. The horrible consequences are twofold: people who can work opt not to work, and a spirit of hatred inevitably emerges in the form of class warfare.

But there does not need to be just one wagon. In the absence of the government's enormous tax-and-spend welfare programs, individuals can address the problem by donating money to solutions they support. Individuals can voluntarily join with others or act on their own to build whatever wagon they think is best, and they can decide who deserves to be in the wagon they are pulling. Loving motives displace coercion. American history is replete with the generosity of Americans for those truly in need. Elitists argue that voluntary approaches come with strings attached, such as pressure to conform to the moral beliefs of donors such as religious groups. The solution is easy: the elitists should make the biggest donations and run their charities the way they think they should be run—and let others do the same.

94. ALL LIVES MATTER

EVERY THREE OR FOUR YEARS, it seems like young liberals come up with a new protest movement to justify gathering together and spending their summers without gainful employment. Occupy Wall Street was a particularly harmless movement. These inarticulate, self-selected critics were unable to convince the country it would be better off without well-developed capital markets.

But then came the Black Lives Matter (BLM) movement. It is clear that blacks suffer disproportionately as victims of crime and that they are disproportionately arrested. But evidence indicates that blacks are not disproportionately killed by police when the data are statistically analyzed to adjust for the fact that blacks tend to have lower incomes and therefore live in high crime areas. I do not see this as a black vs. white issue; it's common sense.

All lives matter, so what could be wrong with claiming that black lives matter? I honestly did not foresee any unintended consequences when the first signs of this well-orchestrated movement emerged. I was wrong. The intelligentsia and political elitists will not acknowledge it, but an increasing body of evidence indicates that an unintended consequence of BLM has been the Ferguson effect. The Ferguson effect means that intense media and government scrutiny of police actions will cause police to be reluctant to intervene in especially dangerous situations, and that the reduced police presence in crime-ridden areas will lead to a spike in crime. These increases in crime will tend to occur in exactly those urban areas that BLM was attempting to help.

In addition to the pressure from government and media, criminal attacks on police officers could have led to having some police officers become less likely to confront criminal activity. Most notably, Micah Xavier Johnson killed five police officers in Dallas during the summer of 2016. Could these events cause police officers to take a less proactive stance against crime?

It would make perfect sense to me, as an economist, if the police officers backed off in dangerous areas. If the perceived costs of doing one's job dramatically increase, the quantity and quality of law enforcement should diminish. If I were a police officer and saw what happened in the media to fellow officers who shot a black person, I would think twice before going into a dangerous inner city where the probability of serious confrontation is higher. And if, to some extent, the police pulled back from dangerous areas of a city, I would expect that criminals would become emboldened in those areas. But logic has been absent from discussion of the Black Lives Matter movement. For example, we know that more than 90 percent of the killings by police are killings of males. Does anyone think the police hate men? Where is the Male Lives Matter movement?

Research by accomplished academics is confirming the hypothesis that serious crime rates increased in urban areas that received increased scrutiny of police relative to other urban areas. It is possible the evidence is faulty. But the potential unintended consequences of the BLM movement are not even part of the discussions on campuses and have only been a minuscule part of the discussion by the media.

Why were the intelligentsia and political elitists so reluctant to explore the potential unintended consequences of the BLM movement? My first explanation was that the media and elitists were concerned that acknowledging the possibility that the BLM movement was provoking violence against police and discouraging law enforcement might discourage free speech. In other words, perhaps the intelligentsia believed that, even if the free speech of the BLM movement caused unnecessary violence, we cannot let that violence silence their voices. That would be a potentially meritorious explanation of the silence.

But then I thought about what has been happening at UC-Berkeley and many other university campuses: conservatives and libertarians are not being allowed to speak in public, supposedly out of fear that people will be hurt during violent protests. The intelligentsia and political elitists are not only silent about the oppression of conservative viewpoints—they oversee the institutions suppressing the free speech. So the principles of free speech are apparently not behind the support that elitists provide to the BLM movement. Could it be that the elitists don't really care that the BLM movement is leading to increased violent crime against blacks if it serves their political purposes? If so, they do not realize that black lives matter.

95. Competition Is Good for the Soul

Communication of honest and accurate information is an essential component of economic efficiency. How can the least-cost methods of production be attained unless decisions are based on reliable information? The problem is that people lie—they lie to others and they lie to themselves. I am no exception.

My senior year in high school was going to be quite special for me. For starters, I was on the swim team, and it looked like I was going to be the fastest in my favorite event: freestyle sprinting. That was until this one guy came along who joined the swim team in November. Within a few months, he took over as our fastest swimmer. I resented his success. Even though he was a nice guy, I wished he would go away. But the truth was I'd become complacent. I had talked myself into believing that I was trying as hard as I could. I was not. I was lying to myself, and I needed a dose of reality.

Some of my students argue that some nations are like my high school nemesis: they are so good at what they do that other nations simply cannot compete with them. They argue that international trade only benefits the most efficient and powerful nations.

But let's set up an extreme case and assume the US is more efficient than Mexico in every industry. Is there anything Mexico could do to benefit from international trade? Yes. Although a better-educated and better-trained workforce is more efficient, it also commands a higher wage. A developing nation can compete by accepting lower wages. That is how nations such as Japan, South Korea, and China became successful. Step 1: Work cheap. Step 2: Become better trained and more efficient and receive better wages. Step 3: Keep learning, earn higher and higher wages, and grow the economy along the way.

In economics we say nations need a *comparative* advantage, not a *competitive* advantage. In other words, do what you're best at doing and, if you accept lower wages, you can successfully compete. Returning to the hypothetical example—even if every Mexican industry is less efficient than America's worst, both Mexico and the US can still benefit from trade. Mexico should focus on what it does well and, by accepting somewhat lower wages than Americans, it will be able to compete successfully against American companies with higher efficiency but higher labor costs. In the long run, Mexico and other nations will gain efficiency, become better producers, and generate higher wages.

Foreign trade does not exploit undeveloped nations; it gives them a chance to thrive. Take China, for example. American colleges and universities used to accept many Chinese students, offering them attractive financial packages because this Asian country's bright and hard-working students could only come if offered such packages. China's economic success has changed that; now many Chinese students come from wealthy families and no longer need financial assistance. China's economy moved away from communism with some important steps toward free enterprise, and the country has demonstrated its ability to compete in international markets. This has unleashed the talent of its people, which has dominoed into more wealth for more Chinese citizens.

More generally, international trade allows every nation to understand how to better direct and develop its energies and talents. Years ago, lobbying by US car makers limited Americans' access to foreign automobiles through tariffs and other trade barriers. Eventually, those trade barriers were lowered, and Americans enjoyed the right to buy cars from any manufacturer in the world. If it were not for these reduced trade barriers, we would all still be driving cars that broke down frequently, needing constant maintenance. But the superiority of foreign cars won out and US automobile manufacturers responded by improving their products so they could compete with foreign manufacturers—a win-win situation for Americans.

Nevertheless, special interests continue to assail international trade and demand protection from competition. But, if international trade is bad, why stop protectionism there? Why not oppose interstate trade? How about opposing inter-county and inter-city trade? That is where the movement to "buy local" is headed. Trade barriers are a bad idea; it is just special interests using government force to receive special treatment.

International competition is good for our economy, just as competition serves a valuable role in our personal lives. My high school nemesis didn't ruin my life. He caused me to face the truth. He showed me that I needed to work harder and smarter. I carried those lessons with me to college (where I set a school swimming record) and beyond. His excellence made my life better, just as competition from home and abroad forces us to deliver higher quality products at attractive prices.

96. SOCIALISTIC SOCIETIES HAD MORE TO FEAR THAN FEAR ITSELF

I SPENT A SHORT AMOUNT of time in Poland in the 1970s when it was under Communist control and again in the late 1990s when it was relatively free. I noticed a huge economic difference on the second trip. The difference was clear from the air as the plane approached Warsaw: new, brightly painted buildings. Downtown Warsaw had large stores stuffed with attractive merchandise and filled with eager shoppers. Decades earlier, there were mostly dismal shops with empty shelves. My mother, who lived there briefly in the 1970s, told me the key to shopping in Poland was to jump into any line that was forming before it got long. A growing line was the sign that the store had received a shipment of something worth buying. During the communist years, there were a few state-run *Pewex* stores that had nice merchandise—but you could only make purchases with foreign currencies. Polish citizens often received these "hard" currencies from relatives in the West, so these stores were created by the government as a way of encouraging citizens to import the currency and spend it with the government.

In a communist country, there are so many rules to control the economy that poor people inevitably find themselves on the wrong side of the law. In Poland, people were not free to work when and how they wished. With such overwhelming poverty, most people cheated one way or another. Perhaps a dentist took care of some patients at home on the weekend. Or someone sold sewing services. Others might raise a pig or some chickens. With so many rules, virtually everyone was breaking at least one. But, by breaking one of these economic rules, a citizen ran the risk of getting in deep trouble if they also criticized the government or a party official. The government would ostensibly punish them for breaking the economic rule when, in truth, the government was quelling criticism directed at the government. The economic laws served to stifle political dissent.

I did not realize that people were afraid when I first visited Poland, even though they were unwilling to discuss politics and economics with a stranger like me. When I returned to the country years later, people were so much more willing to engage in political and economic discussions. They told me what had been happening to them. I am reminded of a joke Ronald Reagan used to tell: An American brags to a Russian that in America a citizen has the right to stand in front of the White House and shout, "To hell with Reagan." The Russian replies: "So what? In Russia, we can stand in front of the Kremlin and yell, 'To hell with Reagan,' too."

But freedom of expression, even in America, is under siege. Discussions in college classrooms have turned into perfunctory exercises in which no one dares say something politically incorrect. The consequences of so-called "hate speech" on campus can be dire and can include mandatory training, suspension, or expulsion.

Corporate America is also feeling the heat. I have noticed that corporate executives increasingly fear doing or saying anything that will upset a high-level government official. The executives make donations to politicians because somewhere, somehow their corporation might be found to have violated one of the millions of regulations. Executives do not want to fall out of favor with government officials because the officials can punish them for violating some obscure regulation. As America's federal, state, and local governments pass more and more intrusive laws to micromanage the lives of its citizens, we will see more and more ordinary people afraid to be open and honest for a similar reason.

Why is it so important that people be free of fear of their own government? Innovation is an engine of economic growth. Fear crushes innovation like kryptonite weakened Superman because innovation requires confidence and ego, and people who live in fear tend to deflate. Our leaders need to instill confidence in those who create. Increasingly they do the opposite. In a speech in 2012, Barack Obama commented, "If you've been successful, you didn't get there on your own." He added, "If you've got a business—you didn't build that. Somebody else made that happen." The threat is clear; you did not build your business, you do not own that business, and we have the moral right to take it away from you if do not cooperate with us.

97. WHEN SHARING IS NOT CARING

IN SOME CLASSES, I MAKE an offer to my students, who tend to underestimate the power of self-interest. I offer them the opportunity to form "grade co-ops." I explain that a grade co-op would consist of two or more students who agree that their grades would reflect the average performance of all the students in their co-op. Everyone in each co-op would get the same grade regardless of their individual performances. I make it clear that, if they form a co-op, they can't quit the co-op under any circumstances. At first, students are excited about the idea. But soon they see potential problems. In all the years I've offered this opportunity, I've only had one student want to form a co-op. Nobody else would join him.

The students know something important about small groups. For years prior to my class, they've been involved in group projects in which some of the students freeloaded off the hard work of the others. They want no part of it for their grade in my class.

Extreme socialism is a large-scale co-op—and it fails on a large scale. Extreme socialism never thrives, but it can survive when the government doesn't allow people to leave.

Moderately socialistic economies such as in Europe and South America fail in slow motion. The buildings have grown old and their standard of living has stagnated. Take Greece, where I spent some wonderful months teaching. I loved much about that country, but the waste dismayed me. One after another, each sector of the economy went on strike and clogged the streets until the workers' leaders reached a compromise with their socialist government on new wages and working rules.

Moderately socialistic economies don't decay quickly for several reasons. First, when other economies—like China—move toward free markets, they generate economic growth that spills over into other economies. Also, nonsocialist countries constantly create new technologies that spur economic growth throughout the world. Finally, the market prices generated in free economies signal to other economies how to better evaluate the benefits and costs of the decisions they face daily. But, even with all these benefits of living amid freer economies, the moderately socialistic countries cannot consistently grow and thrive as much as countries with free markets.

The intelligentsia argue that free market economies aren't always the most successful—and they cite an example or two as if a few examples outweigh the preponderance of the evidence. Most people see what they wish to see. But why do elitists *want* free economies to fail? Elitists have a fondness for central planning because they hope they can be part of the elite group that runs the economy.

The *Wall Street Journal* and the *Heritage Foundation* annually publish an excellent and comprehensive source of information—the *Index of Economic Freedom*. This report measures the state of economic freedom in the world (preview: it's increasing) and how well economic freedom promotes economic prosperity (preview: a lot).

Even though my students refuse to form grade co-ops, some of them cling to the cherished belief that socialism creates utopian lifestyles. For years, I've offered to pay for any student in my class with socialist leanings to move to Cuba or North Korea if they would agree to stay there and never vote in an American election. No one has expressed any interest in accepting my offer. I doubt any elitists would, either.

98. THE PRICE IS USUALLY RIGHT

A FUNNY COMMERCIAL YEARS AGO illustrated a safety feature that caused a car's horn to beep when a tire being inflated reached the proper air pressure. The beep signaled to the person inflating the tires that it was time to stop. But, instead of showing a person inflating the tires of a car, the commercial showed a man on the brink of making a series of faux pas. In each case, when the man did something stupid, he heard a car horn signal that he should stop. In one spot, he shook the hand of his boss too vigorously; in another, he was about to kiss a woman too aggressively, etc.

The commercial noted how nice it would be if life offered this feature. But that is basically what we have: tens of thousands of market prices guiding us to avoid making mistakes, just like the car horn signal.

If I'm offered ten ounces of silver for one ounce of gold, I don't need to be a metallurgist, a miner, or a geologist to know which to take. I just need to know the market prices of the two metals. Owning the commodity with the higher price offers me better opportunities than owning the commodity with the lower price. For example, if the ounce of gold is more valuable, I should keep it because, even if I like silver more than gold, I can sell the gold at its market price, buy the silver at its market price, and pocket the difference.

Our economic lives consist of a series of decisions about which actions will benefit us more than they cost us. The signals we use are market prices. Market prices signal information to the entire world. To know what's valuable and what's not, we don't usually need to know how something was made, how long it took to make it, how precious the materials were that went into making it, or the abilities and preferences of the people who made it. All we need to know is its price. When everyone makes decisions based on market prices, we act in harmony with everyone else's abilities and preferences, and our actions reflect the costs of producing an item.

But how can we know market prices perfectly indicate the true costs and values of the items? The truth is that they don't. In a complex and constantly changing world, no pricing system can always, continuously, and perfectly reflect the true costs and values of every item. But markets do this better than any other system—way better than a government committee.

When people can transact freely in markets, they buy items that have attractive prices, find ways to produce and sell items that appear to command high prices, avoid purchasing overpriced items, and stop producing items that have such low prices they cannot be made at a profit. Every time a price gets out of line with its costs of production, it gets driven back in line by the forces of supply and demand. And, since costs of production ultimately come down to the talents and preferences of producers, everybody's decisions collectively guide market prices to reflect the talents and preferences of producers and consumers throughout the world. It is a "what you know" economy, not a "who you know" economy.

99. Imitation Can Be the Surest Form of Theft

I KNOW A YOUNG ENGINEER who works for an American manufacturer of large metal equipment. One day, a corporate customer shipped back a piece of equipment, complaining that it was poorly made and had broken. As the young engineer and his colleagues inspected the broken piece of equipment, they noticed an unusual mark molded in the metal. The mark was not supposed to be on the equipment they manufacture. It was a letter with a circle around it. It took a while but, eventually, the engineers figured it out. The mark was a symbol on their blueprints providing information about the equipment but was never intended to appear on the finished product. A foreign manufacturer had stolen the blueprints for the equipment and had molded the blueprint symbol into the metal, unaware that the mark was for informational purposes only. The foreign firm was making cheap knock-offs of American-designed products and undercutting the American firm through lower prices. They were using deceit to sell flawed products by riding on the reputation produced by the American firm.

Countries with highly advanced industries are rightfully concerned with industrial espionage, theft of technology, and infringement on patents and trademarks. I spent a little time in communist Poland (1978–79) when my father was hired to help Poland upgrade the technology of one of its manufacturers. It was sad to see a nation with such a proud tradition of engineering talent falling behind in technology due to the flaws in their economic system (communism). I observed what appeared to be blatant attempts to copy products from the West.

Free nations were rightfully concerned with industrial espionage by communists in previous decades. But the biggest thing I have learned from my economic studies is that technological blueprints are not the biggest assets of a free market. The biggest asset is the information contained in market prices. Free markets allow people to communicate their skills and desires. Market prices are the quickly-changing blueprints of efficient economies!

Centrally planned economies and the economies of moderately socialistic nations cannot compete on their own. Those economies rely on observing the prices of goods that arise in free markets to make their decisions. Market prices inform them of the true value of all the resources outside their areas of expertise.

Suppose a firm determines that adding a tiny amount of platinum would lower the amount of energy needed to make a product. Are the energy savings worth the added cost? The firm can compare the price of platinum to the price of energy to find the answer. If the prices are misleading, the decision will be flawed. The prices arbitrarily set by a government committee will be misleading—if not now, at some point in the future when conditions change. Prices in a free market are forced over time to reflect underlying economic realities of scarcity and abundance.

Benefit-cost analyses are only as good as the prices they're based on. In our rapidly changing world, government committees cannot set prices that are as useful as those generated by free markets. Why? Because prices in a free market are challenged every day by thousands of investors and speculators who are searching for underpriced items to buy and overpriced items to sell. Their actions drive prices toward values that rapidly reflect information from throughout the economy.

The key to this process is that the brightest and hardest-working market participants tend to make money by buying underpriced assets and selling overpriced assets. Traders making profits can afford to take bigger risks and, in so doing, they exert greater influence on market prices, while those who lose money leave the market. In a free market the most capable traders, analysts, speculators, investors, and entrepreneurs drive market prices while, in a centrally planned economy, the most politically shrewd bureaucrats control the prices.

The technological advances of free market economies don't occur because our scientists are more intelligent or luckier. They occur because political freedom liberates the mind to be creative, economic freedom incentivizes people to innovate, and free markets provide the communications network to facilitate cooperation on a mass scale.

100. SPECULATORS AND RATS

OUR SOCIETY FREQUENTLY ACCUSES SPECULATORS of causing financial crises and then exploiting those crises for their own benefit.

The first issue is whether speculators cause crises. Where we see a financial crisis, we usually see a lot of speculative activity. But that may be mere correlation, not causality. By analogy, wherever we find lots of garbage, we are likely to find rats, but rats do not create garbage. And, if garbage is properly contained, we are unlikely to find rats. Clearly rats don't cause garbage to exist; it's the other way around. In this analogy, speculators play the rats, which many think fitting. But, if speculators are rats, they're good rats (supposing such a thing exists). The role of speculators in our economy isn't harmless; it's highly beneficial.

Speculation is a contest of survival of the fittest. A speculator makes money by buying low and selling high. The act of buying low and selling high stabilizes markets. When speculators believe a price has fallen too low, they buy, thereby causing the price to stop falling or begin rising. Conversely, when speculators believe a price has risen too high, they sell (or short-sell), which tends to stop the price from rising or even causes the price to fall to a more appropriate level. Therefore, successful speculators stabilize markets.

Speculators who buy high and sell low lose money and eventually go out of business. So, in the long run, speculation helps stabilize markets. In a free market, speculation is dominated by proven winners who put their own money at risk to buy underpriced assets and sell overpriced assets. The idea that speculation reduces long-term market volatility is backed up by most (but not all) of the research on the subject. The number of real crises in modern times is not high enough to generate enough data for conclusive tests, so we should rely more on reasoning and common sense.

Speculators continuously monitor markets for prices that appear too high or too low and then put their own money at risk trying to buy low and sell high. To the extent that they are correct, professional speculators tend to keep prices in line with economic reality. Although speculators only want to serve themselves, they help everyone in the economy. Whenever we want to invest extra cash or liquidate investments to obtain cash, we can have confidence that we're paying or getting a reasonable price on the transaction. That's because the prices of the assets we buy and sell are driven toward rational levels by speculators.

Few opponents of speculation understand the role of speculators in providing liquidity. When an investor wants to buy or sell a stock or other asset, he or she needs to find someone who wants to do the reverse. Another investor might happen to come along at just the right time, which means the two investors can trade with each other. But most of the time, it will be a short-term trader—a speculator—who provides the liquidity we need. Speculators are usually the people who offer us the highest price when we go to sell an investment and the lowest price when we go to buy one. When that is not true, we simply buy or sell with someone else.

Speculators don't cause financial crises; on the contrary, they stave them off. The best speculators exit the market if it gets overpriced, keeping a lid on bullish sentiment, and enter the market when it gets underpriced, preventing investor sentiment from getting too bearish.

It's not just speculators that get blamed for market volatility. Some say that the cause of the crisis of 2007–2009, in particular, was powerful financial executives and wealthy investors who are now gleefully counting all the money they made at the expense of the little guys. But the crisis devastated far more of the wealthy than it benefited. Several large banks, insurance companies, and brokerage firms went out of business. Almost every major bank, insurance company, and brokerage firm saw its stock price drop by at least half. Many were rescued by the private sector (which is what should happen in a free market) or by the public sector (which is crony capitalism). If politicians think a firm is worth rescuing, they should use their own money, not ours.

To be sure, a few people and institutions made money on the crisis, either through luck or skill. But the crisis harmed many speculators, most financial executives, and nearly all investors. Most of the executives devastated by the crisis had nothing to do with causing it. Imagine how it must feel to have lost most of your money and your job, and then be blamed for having caused the crisis and accused of having benefited from it.

101. Bedrooms and Boardrooms

I TALKED OFTEN ABOUT SEX in my classes. The real reason is most intelligent students today have a pretty good idea of what they believe with regard to sex—and I agree with them. They believe their sex lives are nobody's business except their own. And every one of them believes they should have the right to select their intimate relationships based on issues such as gender, race, sexual preference, and physical abilities. They especially believe it's none of the government's business as long as they're adults acting voluntarily.

I challenge students to explain why they have entirely different beliefs when it comes to financial matters. Why should anything two or more people do that involves money be the business of anyone else and the government in particular? Why should monetary transactions be taxed and regulated but not sexual activities? Why should rich people be forced to give money to poor people, but beautiful people not be forced to make love to ugly people?

In the last century, the government has increasingly abandoned its micromanagement of our sex lives, just as it has abandoned its prohibitions on obscene speech and its invasions of other civil liberties. But its involvement in our economic lives has exploded.

In the early 20th century, the federal government levied no income tax. Aside from state taxes in some states, a person offered $100 in pay received a pay envelope with $100 in it. Today, deductions from their income are massive and can include federal income, state income, local income, Social Security, Medicare, and unemployment taxes. The bulletin boards near the human resources area of an organization display many notices of outrageous government mandates from Washington, DC, as well as the state capital, regarding the employer-employee relationship.

I see no difference between regulating behavior in the bedroom and regulating it in the boardroom. I see no essential difference between sexual activity and economic activity. Some students have suggested that I reconsider that viewpoint.

102. Liberals in Action Can Be Worse Than Liberals' Inaction

THE PROGRESSIVE LEFTISTS THAT DOMINATE many American college campuses are busy harassing conservatives rather than policing their own ranks. The witch hunt against conservatives has spawned a wave of faked hate crimes committed by liberals to rally support for their causes. For example, the *Los Angeles Times* reported on August 19, 2004, that a visiting psychology professor at Claremont McKenna College was convicted of filing a false police report. The professor, a convicted shoplifter, reported that her car had been damaged and her $500 briefcase (and other items) had been stolen—an apparent hate crime against a liberal—one who apparently prefers a $500 briefcase to helping the poor. The college community went into mourning. The administration canceled classes the next day at five of the colleges that form the Claremont Colleges. It turned out that the professor had damaged her own car to garner sympathy for the plight of liberals.

I know of this event because my son was one of the students who lost a day of classes while the leftists made speeches decrying the sad state of affairs. When the entire fiasco was revealed as a criminal hoax, the reaction of the leftist campus leaders was muted. Here's the point: Academic elitists enthusiastically shut down campuses and berate students when they believe a crime has been committed against one of their liberal professors. But, when they make a false accusation against innocent students, nothing more is said: "Never mind. Nothing to look at here. Move along."

The instances of similar false hate crimes against liberals on American campuses are numerous. I understand that, with billions of people in the world, virtually every group has its lunatic extremists. My objection is when the majority of the members of a group do not express outrage when the lunatics of their group hurt others. Instead, they usually exploit the events as opportunities to advance the cause of the lunatics and condemn those who oppose them, claiming that these lunatics were driven into their criminal activities by the injustices they faced.

103. BITING THE HAND THAT FEEDS THEM

ONE OF THE MOST PATHETIC displays of economic ignorance and hypocrisy was the Occupy Wall Street protest movement and similar more recent anti-trade protest movements. Years ago, I spent a lot of time at a bank near Wall Street measuring its financial risks. I saw the protests. These naïve young men and women had absolutely no idea of how an economy works and the vital role played by financial and capital markets such as those on Wall Street.

I often smelled another market when I walked to the southeast end of Wall Street. About five blocks north of Wall Street is Fulton Street, home to the Fulton Fish Market until it moved in 2005. The Fulton Fish Market has served as a massive wholesaler of fish, facilitating the distribution of vast quantities and types of fish, supplied via fishing boats, to restaurants and other retailers. No one walking near that market could avoid the reality of what was happening in that market, especially on a hot day when the odors were especially powerful. You could see the trucks and the workers.

There are two key roles that fish markets play: one is matching sellers (suppliers) of fish with buyers (consumers) of fish. The other key role is price revelation. Well-functioning markets generate prices that suppliers and consumers can use to guide their production and consumption decisions. How can fishing boat captains or seafood retailers make wise decisions if they cannot obtain reliable price information? Market prices are the lifeblood of economic cooperation.

Obviously, every economy needs well-functioning food markets to feed its population efficiently. But do large, modern economies need financial markets? "No," according to the young, confident protesters occupying Wall Street. The truth is that all vibrant, modern economies need financial markets. Impoverished nations lack them.

Matching the suppliers of capital with the entrepreneurs who deploy capital is a vital role played by modern capital markets. A less obvious but equally important role of financial markets is that they reveal the price of money (the time value of money indicated by interest rates) as well as the price of bearing financial risks. Efficient decision-making requires reliable prices: reliable prices for labor, for goods, and even for capital.

Fish are tangible. Fish markets smell. The movement of fish from water to boat to market to retailer to table can be observed, understood, and appreciated. Capital is invisible and less likely to be understood and appreciated. To those prone to "fixed-pie" thinking and jealousy, financial markets are just places with highly-paid workers wearing expensive clothing who appear to be producing nothing. Money cannot be "smelled." No one can see money move from wage earner to investment fund to operating firm, and then to the assets that allow a modern economy to exist. But that does not diminish the crucial importance of financial markets to the economies that generate the myriad of miraculous goods and services we enjoy today.

Here is the irony. The Occupy Wall Street protesters relied on a modern economy to keep them fed, clothed, transported, and sheltered. It is a modern economy that keeps them alive as they idle away month after month without producing anything. The anti-trade protesters travel the US and even the entire world to throw rocks through windows, block traffic, set cars on fire, and otherwise try to halt productivity and destroy the creation of wealth. They are biting the hand that feeds them.

104. TECHNOLOGY FAILS

ADVANCES IN TECHNOLOGY HAVE BEEN the driving force behind the doubling of human lifespans and other tremendous accomplishments. If economic freedom is allowed to persist, soon technology will triple human lifespans compared with a few centuries ago.

But economic breakthroughs eventually become wastes of money. Great firms like Woolworths displaced expensive small stores that did not allow customers to touch the merchandise. Kmart and other innovators came along and displaced Woolworths. Then came Walmart. If economic freedom persists, eventually Walmart will be destroyed by Amazon or some other retailing concept that is better.

Technology evolves just as species evolve, to a large extent by trial and error and by survival of the fittest. For economic advances to dominate declines, there must be some mechanism by which good ideas are successfully distinguished from bad ideas.

A famous saying is that a sports team gets better or gets worse, but it never stays the same. That is also true for an economy. The technology that drives the efficiency of a modern economy either progresses or decays. So the key to economic growth is the extent to which its technologies are advancing. The key to technological advances is economic freedom: access of citizens to markets, ability to communicate freely, and confidence that if they create value, they will benefit substantially.

Many people think that America has enough wealth and therefore they strive to protect the old economic ways and the old jobs. If successful in suppressing economic change and technological innovations, they will not only prevent economic growth, they will cause economic decline. But worse than causing economic declines would be the unintended consequence of preventing society from enjoying unknown advances that would have occurred if people had been allowed to remain free.

Brilliant author Ayn Rand wrote a short book (*Anthem*) that opened with the premise that technology and productivity can devastatingly decline when collectivism forces out individualism. When I first read *Anthem*, I thought Rand's point was exaggerated. But, when I observe countries such as Venezuela spiraling into chaos, poverty, and authoritarianism due to collectivism, her words ring true. The capabilities of Venezuela and other such countries actually reverse and decline; these countries find themselves less and less able to perform tasks that were being easily accomplished a decade or two ago, such as pumping oil out of the ground.

The way free markets and individuality promote progress is that they destroy most innovations (the bad ones) and destroy efforts to maintain the status quo. This is good. Most entrepreneurial ideas are bad and need to be destroyed. More importantly, most ideas that were once good—such as VHS tapes—eventually become second-rate and need to be destroyed, no matter how much those old technologies benefit the wealthy and the workers by staying in circulation. Centrally planned economies cannot differentiate between new ideas that are good and new ideas that are bad. More destructively, they preserve lots of bad ideas that were once good ideas by protecting them and subsidizing them. Economies are full of mismanaged enterprises (e.g., the New York City subway system), especially when they are run by governments. Economic freedom drives economic progress by allowing consumers, not government committees, to determine which technology wins and which loses.

Economic Darwinism does not destroy humans; it nourishes humans by destroying half-baked and inefficient methods. Economic Darwinism has led to huge advances in food production and medicine that have enabled the Earth's population to soar toward 10 billion, a number that decades ago was viewed as being absurdly unsustainable. The alternative to economic freedom is hidden behind the borders of North Korea. The North Korean guards on the borders between North Korea and China are there to prevent North Koreans from fleeing from the exact economic authoritarianism that the American intelligentsia and political elites prescribe for this country.

105. WORKER-RELATED DEATHS

WHY ARE WE ALLOWING THE government to control more and more of our economic lives? One reason is that, when a government program is created to fill a perceived need, it takes on a life of its own with a desire to grow larger and more powerful. Government programs (and not-for-profit organizations) continue to grow, even when the need for the program no longer exists.

For example, the March of Dimes organization was founded in 1938 by FDR (as the National Foundation for Infantile Paralysis) to combat polio. When that mission was made obsolete by polio vaccination, the organization searched for, and eventually found, a new purpose. Some government programs are created for needs that never existed.

Consider occupational safety. Premature death due to accidents was commonplace a century or two ago and is still a problem in undeveloped economies. In the US, accidents involving horses, mines, and fires were commonplace 150 years ago relative to today. However, safety in the US workplace has improved dramatically since the Great Depression as evidenced by the following graph.

Data source: National Safety Council: http://injuryfacts.nsc. org/all-injuries/historical-preventable-fatality-trends/class-of-injury/ accessed 4/11/2018. Graphed by author.

The graph reports government-estimated work-related fatalities per 100,000 workers in the US from 1928-1991. The graph ends at 1991 to avoid a large discontinuity that occurs in the data in 1992 due to a change in the method used in government reports to estimate death rates. By the way, the trend since 1992 is similar to the trend up to 1991: a steady decline in occupational death rates. Wonderful news! Whom or what do we have to thank for this marvelous progress? The intelligentsia loudly proclaim two heroes: government regulations and union membership.

Let's start with union membership. Union membership in the US expressed as a percentage of the workforce has been in steady decline since the 1950s, reaching a decline since then of about 50 percent. So union participation and death rates have been heading in opposite directions for well over 50 years.

Perhaps government regulation should get the credit for the improved safety. Looking at the graph, is there any particular point at which the pattern seems to improve? It is erratic prior to 1940, but after 1940 the decline seems even. After displaying the graph in class, I have asked students to guess which year the federal government's Occupational Health and Safety Administration (OSHA) was established—1930 or 1940 are good guesses because of subsequent drops, but the answer is 1971. Clearly, there is no unusual decline on the graph subsequent to 1971 that indicates a change in the overall pattern.

With death rates declining so steadily in the 30 previous years, what happened in 1971 to cause government leaders to believe that a new agency was needed? The fact is that the decline in work-related deaths in the US mirrors that in other nations that experienced substantial economic growth over the same time period. Wealthy societies solve important problems. Economic growth enables improved solutions.

What changed in 1971 was that occupational safety got caught up in the trend of steadily increasing government intrusion into the economic lives of its citizens. And, despite less and less need for its services, OSHA's intrusion keeps growing. For example, from 2007 to 2017, OSHA's estimated budget grew from $484 million to $595 million, with the number of employees (FTEs) rising from 2,173 to 2,273. Shouldn't government agencies shrink when the need for their services declines?

106. A NATION DIVIDED

AMERICA IS INCREASINGLY DIVIDED. WHAT is the underlying cause? I have heard it characterized as a *City Mouse v. Country Mouse* issue, with citizens of densely populated regions preferring a more socialized or even communal approach to governance and with those from more rural areas preferring individualism and the rule of law based on the Constitution. Others characterize the divisions along lines of race, age, gender, wealth, or intellect.

Liberals and conservatives cannot unite on their view of the poor and struggling because their thinking processes differ too much. They differ on the merit of the free enterprise system because they perceive the world differently. Therefore, liberals and conservatives can never develop unified public policies that are fully satisfactory to each. Their differences are deep.

I believe the clearest cause of this divide is whether one focuses on compassion, people, feelings, and the "here and now," or whether one focuses on productivity, logic, actions, and "consequences through time." Here are my three primary points regarding our national divide:

1. Liberals reject attempts to resolve differences through logical reasoning. When confronted with attempts to establish a clear, rational dialogue, they switch topics and obfuscate the issues with debates about terms (e.g., what is the meaning of is).

2. Conservatives reject attempts to respond emotionally to "in the moment" feelings of community, empathy, and social pressure. When confronted with emotion-based calls for mercy and justice, they only see the long-term negatives.

3. Neither side will ever understand the other because they have different priorities. One is concerned about internally consistent logic; the other is concerned about belonging to a group.

For example, consider the disdain of liberals for corporate executives, entrepreneurs, private equity managers, and merchants who receive tremendous income. While some celebrate these success stories in Horatio Alger style, others vilify the resulting millionaires and billionaires as leeches on society.

Interestingly, people rarely vilify lottery winners, even when the prize exceeds $100 million. Apparently, everyone—liberals included—understand that these winners paid for a ticket, just like millions of others, and they won fair and square. Receiving hundreds of millions of dollars without having created a penny of wealth is not offensive to liberals. I also haven't heard liberals vilify rock stars, professional athletes, famous models, Hollywood stars, or prominent artists for earning tens or hundreds of millions of dollars. It appears that liberals do not mind when highly talented entertainers receive tremendous incomes. So why are liberals so incensed about people who amass wealth through ownership or control of businesses? I believe it is because they do not understand how business makes the pie bigger and they think that, if business owners make more money, it must mean that others make less. That is true of lottery winners—who liberals do not criticize—and not true of entrepreneurs—who liberals attack.

Nevertheless, I believe this spectrum of differences between liberal and conservative viewpoints is healthy and valuable to an economy and a society. But it must be balanced. It seems that, in terms of population, the last few presidential elections indicate the balance is near 50/50, which is good.

Perhaps America should embrace the near-even split as being healthy and change from an attitude of conquering each other to compromising with each other. Returning the powers unconstitutionally usurped by the federal government to the people and the individual states would be a good start. Let the liberals run California, New York, and most of the states on the coasts, and let the conservatives run Texas and most of the states in the middle. The key is for each side to stop meddling in the lives of those who wish to co-exist peacefully.

107. THE BOMBER BOYS' FREE RIDES NOT SO FREE

ECONOMISTS USE SEVERAL FOUNDATIONAL CONCEPTS about human behavior in their teaching and research. For example, they teach that people are utility maximizers, meaning that people are constantly seeking to maximize their happiness over their foreseeable lifetimes. Economists also assume people are rational in taking into account opportunity costs: the loss of their second-best option when they select their best option.

Economists are obsessed with the free-rider problem, where people receive benefits from expenditures made by others while not having to contribute their own funds. An example of the free-rider problem is when some people who give to museums or charities generate benefits other people can enjoy, even though they did not help fund the organizations. Economists also focus on the tragedy of the commons, where people ignore the damage they cause to others when they make decisions that benefit themselves.

I also teach these foundational economic concepts. But I take time to point out a group of people I cannot get out of my head: the American "bomber boys" who manned the airplanes that were crucial to the Allied victory in the European theater of WWII. These men volunteered to serve the cause of freedom under conditions in which death was likely. They committed to embarking on numerous missions, even though a high percentage of them would be killed or captured. Were the bomber boys maximizing their lifelong potential happiness? Were they considering all the alternatives they could have selected? Did they mind that many others were acting as free riders? Did they abandon their posts and cause a tragedy of the commons? No. They gave their lives for their love of freedom and their commitment to the ideal that governments that wish to enslave people must not be allowed to rule the world.

Economists also teach that sunk costs should be ignored. In other words, once a cost has been paid, it should not be considered when making new decisions involving future benefits and costs. Our intelligentsia seem perfectly capable of throwing away the liberties for which so many young Americans died. Perhaps they view the deaths of these war heroes as sunk costs. However, I cannot stop admiring the sacrifices made for us by these freedom lovers who died that others might live in liberty.

108. WORLD-CLASS WELFARE

ACCORDING TO MACROECONOMISTS, THERE ARE two major determinants of economic growth: demand and money. I believe that macroeconomists as a group tend to be wrong. It has been said that God invented macroeconomists so that weather forecasters would not look so bad.

Let's start with demand. The famous economist John Maynard Keynes claimed that economies thrive or languish based on the society's aggregate demand for production. Keynes focused on stimulating demand through government spending. The idea is that government can stimulate and moderate growth by adjusting the government's spending levels. According to Keynesian economists, high government spending during slowdowns can spur demand, which multiplies through the economy as consumers spend their newly found wealth.

But, in the long run, government spending takes money out of the pockets of consumers meaning that, in the long run, government spending impedes economic growth. As proof, note that those economies where the government hogs the most goods and services languish the most severely.

The famous economist Milton Friedman argued that the availability and cost of credit (borrowing) and money was the key to real, sustained economic growth. Friedman should be credited with emphasizing the importance of controlling inflation so that people would have a reliable currency with which to trade and plan. But a nation's economic prosperity is not a simple function of monetary policy. People can barter or establish their own currencies (e.g., Bitcoin). Venezuela has devastating inflation, and its pathetic currency hurts the economy, but it is not the primary problem there. Even if Venezuela instantly switched to allowing prices and trading using US dollars, it would still languish.

I believe that an economy's vitality is driven by the society's institutions, particularly the extent to which most citizens believe they have the opportunity to be productive and that being productive is the surest way to prosper. It is just common sense. The whole of an economy is comprised of the sum of its parts. In order to increase the total hours of hard and smart work performed, individuals must work hard and make good decisions. They do not need government telling them when to work hard and how to work smart. They simply need to believe that, if they work hard and smart, they will be appropriately rewarded.

Governments that allow economic freedom, supporting private property rights and other natural rights, tend to prosper. Supporting private property rights includes having a legal system that protects the creators of value by allowing them to benefit from most or all of the value they create.

The biggest deterrents to economic prosperity are:

1. When governments prevent some of its people from creating value by protecting its cronies from competition;

2. When government allows others to steal money or other assets from those who create the value; and,

3. When government takes money from those who create value and gives it to people who are not creating value (welfare).

America treads down the disastrous path of socialism when the government takes money from its best value creators (i.e., highest taxpayers) and gives it those Americans who would prefer to live off the government's largess. Worse, America leads the entire world down the path to poverty when it implements socialism on a global scale by taking money from our most productive citizens (i.e., highest taxpayers) and giving it to nations that hate America. It is welfare on a global scale.

Let's turn to America's foreign aid policies. I am appalled that the US government provides assistance (according to www.washingtonpost.com accessed 4/13/18) as follows, in order:

Afghanistan	$4.7B
Israel	$3.1B
Egypt	$1.5B
Iraq	$1.1B
Jordan	$1.0B
Pakistan	$0.7B

The next four countries that complete the list are African nations.

I cannot think of a list of nations that, when viewed as a whole, are doing less to better themselves. I remember reading in a newspaper several years ago about a local high school football program in which many of its best athletes got into trouble for off-the-field problems such as theft and underage drinking. One of its football coaches lamented to the newspaper reporter with something to effect of: "I cannot understand why these players would do these things and disrespect our school so badly—we give them every opportunity and everything they could ask for."

How much more money will the US government take out of the pockets of America's value creators and give it to nations that hate us, disrespect us, wallow in their dysfunctions, and work against us in virtually every way possible?

109. IDENTITY POLITICS

THROUGHOUT HISTORY MANY PEOPLE, PERHAPS most, have formed their belief systems through identity politics, the process whereby people adopt political ideologies based on a desire to belong to a group of people that helps them feel good. It is dangerous. Nazi Germany exemplifies identity politics. In the late 1970s, I toured the Auschwitz concentration camp in southern Poland where it is estimated that more than one million people died. It is heart-wrenching to witness the evidence of the multitude of innocent families that were destroyed, all of which began with a movement based on a charismatic leader, a well-organized political party, and identity politics.

There is a better way: basing one's life on a belief system supported by reason and evidence. In many classes, I've begun a discussion of corporate ethics by placing my belief system with regard to ethics on the board in one line:

I believe it is wrong to initiate—or threaten to initiate—force, fraud, or violence against anyone else.

Few students agreed, yet none offered an alternative or had even seen a concise alternative.

Modern societies thrive from basing their institutions on these beliefs. The intelligentsia and political elite reject my belief system because they cannot stand the idea of allowing others to live free from their control. They think they are logical and that their ideas will generate successful outcomes. But they refuse to even engage in logical and evidence-based discussions with the people that oppose them. Try it sometime if you disagree. Find a specific belief that a liberal espouses and that conflicts with reasoning or evidence. Then try to get the liberal to discuss the topic all the way to a logical conclusion. They will not do it. If they cared about being logical or factually correct, they would not be a liberal on economic issues.

The belief systems of the intelligentsia and political elites have not generated successful outcomes for anybody other than the leaders of the movements. Collectivism and multi-culturalism have not succeeded on an involuntary basis or in large scale. The past is littered with failed economies that attempted long-term voluntary collectivism. Today, economies such as those in Venezuela, Cuba, and North Korea only limp along based on trade with other economies. The Heritage Foundation publishes data and analyses that show the long-term negative effects of collectivism on economic growth. Collectivism and multi-culturalism can only survive with authoritarianism. And societies do not flourish in the long run under authoritarianism.

Also consider the logical contradictions and hypocrisy of the belief system of the intelligentsia and political elite. They believe everyone has the right to engage in a mutually agreed upon intimate social relationship with any person of their choice regardless of race, sexual preference, religion, economic background, and so forth. But they despise and outlaw any attempt of a person to be similarly selective in economic decisions, such as which customers to serve and which people to select as employees. And all liberals believe they should have the right to select their intimate relationships based on issues such as gender, race, sexual preference, and physical characteristics.

The rules do not apply to the intelligentsia and political elites. They only make sure that their servants are legally paid and documented when they decide to run for public office. They impose the TSA on the masses, but insist that the TSA not control their access to their private jets. Suppression and even extermination of the undesirables and the deplorables, will be the tragic end result of identity politics run amok, because a movement void of reason and evidence that has power will apply those powers with their most base instincts.

110. GREED IS NOT GOOD; IT IS GREAT

ONE OF MY FAVORITE DISCUSSION questions in class is the following. Assume there are two identical twin brothers, Gordon and Angel, who have equal skills, abilities, and everything else except for one thing: Gordon is obsessed with accumulating wealth, while Angel is obsessed with helping the poor. How will the decisions of these brothers differ when they order food at a restaurant (i.e., consume) or select a career (i.e., produce)?

Let's start with how Gordon and Angel might differ in what food they order at a restaurant. With Gordon so obsessed with accumulating wealth, he would likely order one of the cheapest things on the menu. He might like lobster, but he loves money. So he gets a simple sandwich. What about Angel? Angel knows that every penny he spends on food is one less penny he will have to help poor people so he, too, would be drawn toward the cheapest items on the menu. Angel also wants society to expend as few resources as possible in meeting his needs so there will be resources left over to meet the needs of others. Angel also orders a simple sandwich.

It's easy to see that both brothers will spend very little on their own comforts, not just when dining in a restaurant but when spending money anywhere. Both brothers will endeavor to find ways to derive benefits from their purchases, but they will try to do so as cost-effectively as possible. This is good for everyone involved. When we try to obtain personal satisfaction at the lowest cost (whether for selfish reason or not), we are cooperating with society by consuming less of society's resources.

How about their career choices? Many of my students predict that Gordon will try to succeed in a place like Wall Street while Angel will become a social worker or cleric. But Angel becoming a social worker might not make sense if he has the skills to succeed in a lucrative profession. When I taught as a professor at major universities, I met students who were on the verge of becoming well-paid professional athletes. Suppose Angel were an especially talented young athlete who came to me and said, "I love playing my sport and I have been offered a ton of money to go pro. But I want to help the poor, so I plan on quitting my sport and joining the Peace Corps." If helping the poor is really his goal, wouldn't it make more sense for Angel to make a gazillion dollars by going pro and using that money to fund other people to do the charity work? Wouldn't the world be better off if he did what he is best at doing (entertaining people with his athletic talent) and let other people do the charity work—like Gordon, perhaps? The point is that both Angel and Gordon will be drawn toward their highest-paying opportunities, regardless of their degree of altruism.

Free markets encourage people to serve other people as efficiently and effectively as possible. Markets encouraged Michael Jordan to play basketball and, better yet, encouraged him to stop playing baseball. Markets guide people into applying their greatest talents in ways that will create the most benefit for other people. Lots of people enjoyed watching Jordan play basketball. Few enjoyed watching him play baseball. Markets made our lives better by encouraging Michael to entertain us better. And markets encourage Warren Buffet and other talented investors to apply their skills to the economy's most important components in a modern economy that includes its financial system. People have the natural right to pursue careers that pay very little but give them joy. It is a selfish path, but it is their right. People who pursue the highest-paying jobs should be celebrated for creating the most value and paying the highest taxes.

111. A SODA FOR ME AND SOME OATS FOR MY COMPANION

I HAVE A FAMILY FRIEND who periodically needs to fly long distances with the family dog—a big Weimaraner. Recently, he learned that the airline would no longer accept such a big dog, even for a large fee. The dog owner found a way to get around the new rules. With a few clicks on the internet, he was able to buy a therapy dog vest—allowing him to not only to bring the dog on the plane but to do so for free. There seem to be a lot of therapy dogs in airports lately. Therapy dogs are also common now in shopping centers and other public places.

The madness began when people realized judges and juries in America would grant ludicrous awards for punitive damages to the "little guy" based on allegations that a business made a decision that inconvenienced the little guy. Soon Americans began viewing corporations as a cross between an ATM and an indentured servant. "If you do anything to anger me, I will sue you."

With businesses forced to accommodate therapy animals, we have reached a midpoint on this pathway to insanity. The genie is out of the bottle, and there will be no end to the ludicrous demands that will be placed on businesses. But, at some point, even our judicial system needs to draw the line in its efforts to create new rights for people while denying the owners of businesses any rights regarding their property.

The great comedian Lewis Black claims to have overheard a young woman saying the dumbest thing he'd ever heard in his life. She said, "If it weren't for my horse, I wouldn't have spent that year in college." Her statement cannot be too far from saying, "If I can't be with my horse, I won't be able to get on that airplane."

If anyone thinks snakes on airplanes is a scary or stupid idea, the future holds a big surprise, because this crazy society of ours is about to let therapy horses on airplanes.

112. WHO'S TO SAY THAT AMERICA HAS NEVER HAD A FEMALE PRESIDENT?

EARLY ON IN MY 25 years of teaching at a small predominantly liberal arts college, I certainly learned one thing: the most vocal faculty saw no natural difference between men and women, except they grudgingly accepted the differences in genitalia. I learned this mostly from the women's and gender studies majors, obviously experts in the matter. According to them, any perceived differences between the genders are illusions steeped in prejudice or the result of centuries of discrimination in the evil society known as America.

The following phrases became forbidden on campus: "Thinks like a woman," "Acts like a woman," "Dresses like a woman," "Walks like a woman," etc. No one was permitted to contradict or even question these rules.

Imagine my surprise when I began hearing people on campus talk about transgendered people and how, for instance, a biological male should be allowed to select a female restroom if that person viewed himself as a woman, dressing like a woman and acting like a woman. My first reaction was concern: didn't these people advocating for transgendered people realize they were uttering forbidden phrases on campus? Didn't they realize they would soon be punished for their vicious attack on women as a gender group that differed from men? I was shocked when they were celebrated by the intelligentsia! I should have known none of them would get in trouble. They were part of the intelligentsia. Elitists protect each other so their coalition can be strong enough to destroy anyone who disagrees with them, by using accusations of racism, homophobia, misogyny, xenophobia, and the like.

The academic community delved boldly into this great awakening regarding transgendered people, making it the key issue of our times (until Trump was elected). The new dialogue centered on the concept that behavioral gender is valid and biological gender is not, in direct opposition to the previous dialogue that held that there was no such thing as behavioral gender.

This new awakening is headed for a shipwreck if our country accepts that each person is entitled to claim the gender of his or her choice. There is no way to prove a person claiming to think of himself as a woman is telling the truth. This means every biological male will have an undeniable right to demand to be treated as a woman (much like Senator Elizabeth Warren apparently received benefits by claiming to be Native American). This transgender bandwagon could be disastrous for women. What will happen to most women's sports teams if any male claiming to view himself as a woman can compete on any women's sports team and gain equal rights to apply for collegiate athletic scholarships? I suspect the top salaries in the WNBA would soon be held by biological males.

More recently, the idea of fluid gender has been advanced by the intelligentsia. Fluid gender means that people can not only select the gender of their choice, but they can change it through time. How will society provide special protections and accommodations exclusively to women when opportunists can flip the gender switch at will to game the system?

113. CONSERVATIVES AREN'T THE ONLY ENDANGERED SPECIES

MANY STUDENTS TODAY ARE UPSET about endangered species. So I ask my students if they've ever stopped to think about how many cattle are killed in the United States each year. The answer is about 30 percent of the cattle, which is about 40 million per year. Nevertheless, despite tens of millions of cattle being slaughtered each year, the species is not endangered.

Contrast this with a highly endangered species such as the black rhino in Africa. That species has lost more than 95 percent of its population in the last 50 years. The current population has dwindled to less than 3,000 as poachers have slaughtered them for their horns.

But American cattle are also valuable, and people kill about 30 percent of them each year for their meat. Worse yet, the US government supports and facilitates their slaughter through programs such as inspections of meat processing plants. Nevertheless, the population of cattle is stable. Meanwhile, the population of African rhinos is dwindling despite the avowed efforts of African governments to protect them. Why are cattle doing better than rhinos, even though governments are trying to save rhinos and are facilitating the slaughter of cattle? The answer is because self-interest is working harder to keep cattle populations stable while poachers are working very hard to kill rhinos. It is often difficult for a government to control a force as strong as self-interest. The key to saving the rhinos is getting the forces of self-interest on the side of preservation rather than on the side of extinction.

The cattle are privately owned and highly valuable. Therefore, their owners have a tremendous incentive to protect them and ensure that they reproduce adequately to preserve their population.

Rhinos are not privately owned, so there are no owners with a strong financial interest in preserving the species. The more rhinos the poachers harvest, the more money they get. Governments and charitable organizations do not have a strong self-interest in preventing poaching. Note that the more endangered the rhinos become, the more aid money pours into governments and charitable agencies to save the species.

Private ownership and quasi-private ownership, such as by zoos and wildlife refuges, protect hundreds of species from extinction. Large, private hunting preserves in the United States manage their wildlife populations to ensure that they can sustain their source of revenue. These private hunting preserves have the pleasant but unintended consequence that they protect the global populations of certain endangered species. If we allowed private ranchers to own and breed mammals that are being slaughtered by poachers for their tusks, horns, and hides, eventually they would drive the poachers out of business.

That said, extinction of many species happens naturally, predates humankind, and benefits the world through natural selection. Sometimes I suspect that the reason the intelligentsia have failed to reach an agreement as to why so many species of dinosaurs vanished is that they hate to admit that they have not been able to find a way to blame the extinctions on humans.

114. THE PIGS? LET THEM EAT BREAD

FROM 1960 TO 1980, THE Soviet Union found itself unable to grow enough food to feed its people, so every five years the Soviet leadership announced a new plan to grow more food, especially grain. Five-year plans became more and more ambitious as each previous plan failed and the situation worsened. Instead of making progress, the Soviet Union was increasingly unable to feed itself despite a huge workforce and vast quantities of fertile land. By the late 1970s, the Soviet Union needed to import massive amounts of grain.

The Soviet Union was making catastrophic economic decisions. For example, while the Soviet Union as a whole was struggling to produce enough grain to feed its people, individual citizens were feeding bread to pigs. Feeding fresh bread to pigs is insane when people are hungry. Bread comes to consumers by taking one of the most expensive grains (wheat), combining it with yeast, sugar, and butter, baking it, and shipping it to stores. In a free market, bread is quite expensive relative to livestock feed. But, for individual Soviet citizens, buying bread and feeding it to pigs was smart because the price of bread was heavily subsidized by the government. From a macroeconomic perspective, it was a downright stupid way to produce pork.

Even as the Soviets were importing grain and feeding it as bread to pigs, America's intelligentsia and political elites espoused the tremendous benefits of a Soviet-style economy and centrally planned economies in general. They still push for central planning. Why? In a centrally planned economy, the country takes some of its brightest experts from the most prestigious universities and tasks them with making the economy's biggest decisions. Doesn't it make sense that very smart people would make these big decisions better than common people? To the casual observer, a free market economy makes no sense at all because it allows every farmer, manufacturer, miner, service provider, and consumer to do whatever they want, regardless of whether they've even graduated high school.

But Wisdom is justified by her children: centrally planned economies fail while free market economies thrive. Central planners rely on information presented to them using words. Entrepreneurs are forced in a free market to rely on information being presented to them from the actions of buying and selling. People lie to themselves and others using words, but they tend to reveal more honest information in their actions. How can central planners truly know whether all farmers are trying their best to deliver all of their output to the collective? How can central planners truly know whether the reports that they receive accurately report the economic realities? The leaders of centrally planned economies are notorious for fabricating wildly inaccurate statistics on economic productivity and progress. Is there any reason to believe that only the top leaders game the system with inaccuracies?

In a market economy, lowly people acting independently and forced to live with the consequences of their decisions come up with tons of new ideas. These lowly masses experiment with their ideas, and perhaps 99.9 percent of those ideas are bad. The innovators with bad ideas lose wealth and are forced to change their ways or quit. But, occasionally, some of these common people hit on a good idea, even though they did not attend an Ivy League school. If the idea truly is good, it will soar in popularity as other common people see the success and replicate it, driven by their need to stay competitive. But, in a centrally planned economy, when central planners fail, they or their successors are usually given more money and more power to force their old ideas on the masses.

The surprising result is that a few privileged intellectual elites simply can't compete with experimentation on a mass scale. When lowly people are allowed to experiment independently and when a market-based economy forces participants to bear the consequences of their decisions, good ideas win out.

Central economic planning has persisted long-term in countries like North Korea, East Germany, and Cuba because they did not allow their citizens to flee. How can central planning persist for more than a few years in supposedly democratic countries like Venezuela? Sometimes the answer is because of massive natural resources. But often the answer is that the populace keeps hoping that central planning will work, and that the past economic problems will be rectified when the leadership is changed or a few more capitalists have been thrown in jail and had their property nationalized. The intelligentsia believe they are the chosen ones, chosen to force their ideas on others because they are smart and they deserve more power. That is the ultimate escape clause of the intellectual and political elitists: they claim their system ultimately works, but that it just needs to further repress individual choice.

115. CRITICAL THINKING

ACADEMIA CELEBRATES CRITICAL THINKING. OxfordDictionaries. com (accessed 4/21/2018) defines critical thinking as the "objective analysis and evaluation of an issue in order to form a judgement." In my career as a professor, I saw improving the critical thinking skills of my students as a premier goal—perhaps the highest goal. The problem with modern academia is its focus on the *criticism* at the expense of the *thinking*. Academia is the least likely place to find *objective analysis*.

At their core, intellectual elites criticize everything that challenges their authority and support everything that kowtows to their authority. Objectivity pales in comparison to expediency as a guiding principle of the intellectual elite.

For example, the intellectual and academic elites gushed over President Obama. Very early (2009) into President Obama's first term, he was awarded the Nobel Peace Prize for *doing* absolutely nothing. The Nobel Committee cited his "extraordinary efforts"—his calls for nuclear nonproliferation and his reaching out to the Muslim World—as reasons. Yet, *The New York Times* (5/26/2016) reported that the Obama presidency "reduced the nuclear stockpile less than any other post-Cold War presidency." The nuclear threat from North Korea exploded (pun intended) during Obama's presidency. And, during Obama's presidency, the US bombed more countries—especially Muslim countries—than President George W. Bush did. Let's face it; President Obama was awarded the Nobel Peace Prize for being an articulate and politically correct critic.

The intellectual and academic elites do not understand what makes economies in general—and businesses in particular—productive. They only know how to criticize. But they are not even-handed in their criticism. On campus, the only people whose behavior is allowed to be criticized are (1) those who oppose politically correct dogma, and (2) non-liberal, Christian, heterosexual, white males.

116. WAYS TO RUIN AND SAVE AN ECONOMY

THERE ARE MANY WAYS TO kill an economy:

1. Engage in cronyism, which allows government to conspire or partner with major organizations, especially corporations. When governments are allowed to harness their coercive

powers (taxation, fines, regulation, subsidies, protections, etc.) to benefit their friends, supporters, and partners, the game changes from value creation to stealing a bigger slice of a shrinking pie.

2. Attack the value creators, citing their luck and special opportunities. This serves as a foundation for encouraging class warfare by claiming that the increased wealth of entrepreneurs and merchants is coming out of the pockets of people who have no choices and no opportunities.

3. Centralize all major institutions to consolidate large-scale power and eliminate small-scale competition. Examples include the federal government (at the expense of state and local governments), central public school districts, central churches (i.e., united churches controlled by national organizations), massive unions, and huge conglomerate corporations. Government then controls the centralized institutions through massive systems of regulations, rewards, and penalties.

4. Ensure that all major institutions, especially the education and judicial systems, are controlled by the intelligentsia who respond by actively supporting the political elites.

5. Establish massive government programs that take wealth from those who create it and give it to the poor, in return for their votes, of course.

On the other hand, there is only one thing needed to unleash the natural creativity and energy of people:

Strong government institutions with powers limited to protecting the natural rights of its citizens from the leeches and parasites who would steal wealth created by others, allowing everyone, even speculators, traders, and merchants, to keep the value they create to do anything they wish, as long as they do not trample on the natural rights of others.

117. FINAL THOUGHTS ON INEQUALITY

THE DEBATE IN AMERICA OVER income and wealth inequality is filled with nonsense including "equal pay for equal work," and "no employee of an organization should earn more than ten times as much as the lowest paid employee." People spout these propositions about all organizations, many of which they know nothing about.

So let's look at some organizations with economic realities that are quite obvious to the everyone. Professional athletes are doing the same work, whether they play in the major premier leagues or the lowest leagues. Do we really think it is fair to the most talented athletes to force owners to pay all athletes the same salary regardless of their ability to attract spectators? It is obvious that premier athletes in major sports deserve making hundreds of times as much money as ordinary athletes because they attract spectators who are collectively willing to pay hundreds of times as much to watch them. The same is true of the world's premier music groups compared to ordinary music groups: fans will pay hundreds of times more money to attend a world-class concert than to listen to a local band. People going to world-class concerts perceive that the musicians are generating entertainment that is worth hundreds of times more money than the entertainment generated by mediocre musicians, otherwise they would not pay the huge ticket prices.

The same can be said about the relative value produced by premier artists, motivational speakers, authors, fashion designers, models, etc. Doesn't a musician selling hundreds of millions of copies of a song or an author selling millions of books deserve thousands of times more money than a mediocre musician or author selling only a few songs and books?

So what about businesses? Can a firm's most important employee be worth a hundred times more than a mediocre worker? Probably not when it comes to a small firm doing non-technical work, such as a landscaping company. But, in those small firms, the top employee does not earn hundreds of times as much as the lowest worker. But what about a leading tech firm? Didn't Steve Jobs generate hundreds of times more value for society than the entry-level workers at Apple? We know the answer is yes because we understand the innovations he led and how valuable they have been to billions of people. The same is true, perhaps to a lesser degree, among many of the world's largest organizations. The success or failure of creating value in many massive firms hinges on a few top performers, not the entry-level employees.

Do you know anyone who would be willing to get serious medical care from a hospital that offers all of its employees, from surgeons to cafeteria workers, the same salary? Do you know anyone who would be willing to pay as much to attend a middle school soccer game as the World Cup finals? I would like to get those people together and have them pay as much for me to speak to them as they would pay to listen to a Nobel Prize winner!

118. FOR GENERATIONS STILL TO COME...

IN THE 1980s, THE INTELLIGENTSIA and political elitists argued that Reagan's dogmatic beliefs and harsh criticism of dictatorships would send the world spiraling into war. They warned of the dire consequences all through the 1980 presidential election and throughout Reagan's years as president.

Yet on the very day Reagan took his first presidential oath of office, the Iranian government released the 52 remaining American hostages they had held for 444 days. The intelligentsia and political elitists argue that the timing was a coincidence. They argue that the release had been discussed and negotiated prior to the inauguration and was entirely due to the excellent work of President Jimmy Carter. Elitists will believe anything that makes them feel good, irrespective of how much contrary evidence exists. The hostages were released on the day of Reagan's inauguration because the Iranians knew for more than two months there was going to be a "new sheriff in town" starting on that day—one who might not be as easy to push around.

On June 12, 1987, Reagan delivered a speech near the Berlin Wall:

"We believe that freedom and security go together, that the advance of human liberty can only strengthen the cause of world peace. There is one sign the Soviets can make that would be unmistakable, that would advance dramatically the cause of freedom and peace. General Secretary Gorbachev, if you seek peace, if you seek prosperity for the Soviet Union and Eastern Europe, if you seek liberalization, come here to this gate. Mr. Gorbachev, open this gate. Mr. Gorbachev, tear down this wall!"

And the wall indeed came down and, within a decade, former citizens of the Soviet Union were taking my finance course here in America.

Ronald Reagan once proclaimed, "You and I have a rendezvous with destiny. We will preserve for our children this, the last best hope of man on earth, or we will sentence them to take the first step into a thousand years of darkness."

In another speech, Ronald Reagan added, "Freedom is never more than one generation away from extinction. We didn't pass it to our children in the bloodstream. It must be fought for, protected, and handed on for them to do the same, or one day we will spend our sunset years telling our children and our children's children what it was once like in the United States where men were free."

Reagan's two terms in office not only sparked a huge economic turnaround from the previous 15 years of malaise; it laid the foundation for ending the Cold War after more than 40 years. We run the risk of losing both the incredible progress of the last two centuries, but also the unfathomable progress of future centuries. Technological progress is still accelerating with potential breakthroughs in coming decades such as immortality, teleporting, and things we cannot even imagine today.

Reagan correctly saw a link between liberty and the two primary goals of society: prosperity and peace. Rights are the foundation of liberty. It is only through respecting the natural rights of others that we can enjoy long-term prosperity and peace.

ACKNOWLEDGMENTS

FREEDOM FIRST IS THE CULMINATION of an enormous number of delightful hours spent reflecting on and then discussing the qualities that lead to economically prosperous societies. Along the way, I've benefited from the insights of countless leading thinkers regarding economics through their television appearances (e.g., John Stossel), through their lectures (e.g., Russ Roberts), and through their writing (e.g., Thomas Sowell, Don Boudreaux, and Walter Williams). I also learned from the several thousand students with whom I interacted throughout my career as a professor. I now have the privilege of thanking a few people whose contributions to this effort—and my life in general—are especially noteworthy.

First, I am indebted to the Defiance Press & Publishing staff and CEO David Thomas Roberts for their support. Early work on this book benefited greatly from the insights and suggestions of Harry David, while the final draft was wonderfully improved by the careful and talented editing of Lisa Cerasoli and Janet Musick—thank you all.

Throughout my career, I benefited from talented colleagues who fed my intellect such as Brian Aldershof, Seth Anderson, Keith Black, Dan Burnside, Nick Calley, Earl Cantwell, Mark Crain, Nicole Crain, Jack Helmuth, Fluney Hutchinson, Hossein Kazemi, Kristaps Licis, Qin Lu, Jim Miles, Pierre Saint-Laurent, Jim Verbrugge and Randy Woolridge—most of whom have been great friends as well.

I am grateful for the wisdom of Layla Kassem; the steadfast support of Jim Head; the love and encouragement of my extended family, the Claybergers; and to Tyler Vernon and the rest of the group at Biltmore Capital Advisors.

I am especially indebted to Gladstone (Whit) Whitman, a fantastic alum of Lafayette College who passed away in 2018 and to whom this book is dedicated. Whit introduced me to Austrian economics and mentored my understanding of economic behavior through his delightful powers of observation and deduction. Whit inspired me not just regarding economics, but through his courage, dignity, and perseverance.

There are five long-term and especially dear friends to whom I am immeasurably grateful: Rob Gerych, who has modeled a virtuous life since 1976; John Howland, who urged me to write this book and has stood by me since 1978; Nelson Lacey, who has brightened my life since 1982 in ways too numerous to mention; John Zdanowicz, who has been my dear friend and brilliant advisor since 1985; and Michael Kelly, who has shared his tremendous intellect, knowledge, training, and humor with me since 2005. These friendships have been deeper and more wonderful than I ever dreamed possible.

My most profound indebtedness is to my family: my tremendous brother (Dave); my three remarkable children (Rob, Jenny, and Emily); and my brilliant and loving wife, Suzanne. It is their love that sustains me.

While the people I have noted contributed vastly to my ability to write *Freedom First*, flaws undoubtedly remain in the book. Any remaining errors are not the fault of these admirable colleagues, friends, and loved ones—they are the result of a vast left-wing conspiracy.